The Despised and the Damned

The Despised and the Damned:
THE RUSSIAN PEASANT THROUGH THE AGES

JULES KOSLOW

RUSSIA OLD AND NEW SERIES
Jules Koslow, General Editor

The Macmillan Company, New York, New York
Collier-Macmillan Ltd., London

The Macmillan Company
866 Third Avenue, New York, N.Y. 10022
Collier-Macmillan Canada Ltd., Toronto, Ontario

Library of Congress Catalog Card Number: 72–78618

First Printing

Printed in the United States of America

Thou art wretched,
Thou art bountiful,
Thou art mighty,
Thou art impotent,
Mother Russia!

—Nikolai Alekseyevich Nekrasov

We are full of the feeling of national
pride and precisely because we especially
hate our slavish past. . . .

—Vladimir Ilyich Lenin

Contents

1. Early Years — 1
2. The Village — 6
3. The Mir — 11
4. The Landowner — 19
5. The Peasant — 31
6. Economy and Work — 36
7. The Family — 49
8. The Peasant Condition — 55
9. Customs — 62
10. The Peasant Character — 71
11. Religion, the Church, and Superstition — 84
12. Flight and Migration — 92
13. The Peasant in the City — 96
14. Emancipation — 100
15. Post-Emancipation — 106
16. The New Politics and the Peasant — 112
17. The Years Before the 1917 Revolution — 118
18. Revolution, Civil War, and Reconstruction — 126
19. The Drive Toward Collectivization — 135
20. The Collective and State Farm — 141
21. The New Soviet Peasant — 153
   Bibliography — 165
   Index — 167

The Despised and the Damned

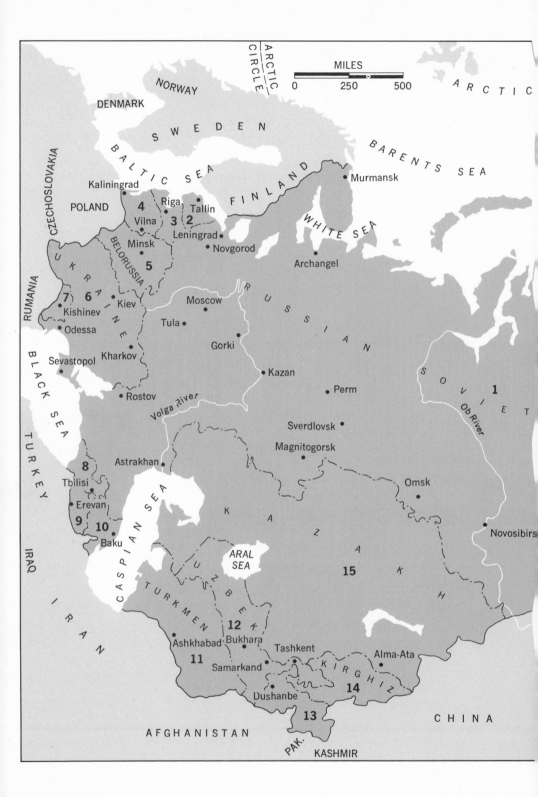

MILES

0   250   500

ARCTIC CIRCLE

NORWAY

DENMARK

SWEDEN

BALTIC SEA

FINLAND

BARENTS SEA

ARCTIC

WHITE SEA

• Murmansk

CZECHOSLOVAKIA

POLAND

Kaliningrad •

Riga •

4

Vilna •

Tallin •

3 **2**

Leningrad •

• Novgorod

• Archangel

Minsk •

5

BELORUSSIA

UKRAINE

R U S S I A N

S O V I E T

7
Kishinev •

6

Kiev •

• Moscow

• Tula

• Gorki

RUMANIA

• Odessa

• Sevastopol

Kharkov •

• Kazan

Ob River

1

BLACK SEA

• Rostov

Volga River

• Perm

• Sverdlovsk

TURKEY

8
Tbilisi •

Astrakhan •

• Magnitogorsk

• Omsk

• Novosibirs

• Erevan

9

10

Baku •

CASPIAN SEA

K A Z A K H

ARAL SEA

IRAQ

UZBEK

15

IRAN

TURKMEN

Ashkhabad •

12
Bukhara •

Tashkent •

• Alma-Ata

KIRGHIZ

11

Samarkand •

14

Dushanbe •

13

AFGHANISTAN

PAK.

KASHMIR

CHINA

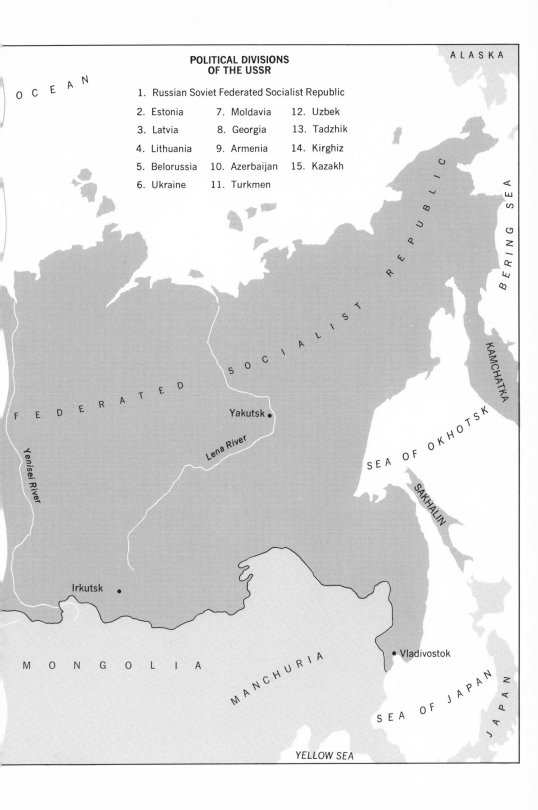

**POLITICAL DIVISIONS
OF THE USSR**

1. Russian Soviet Federated Socialist Republic
2. Estonia
3. Latvia
4. Lithuania
5. Belorussia
6. Ukraine
7. Moldavia
8. Georgia
9. Armenia
10. Azerbaijan
11. Turkmen
12. Uzbek
13. Tadzhik
14. Kirghiz
15. Kazakh

OCEAN

ALASKA

BERING SEA

FEDERATED SOCIALIST REPUBLIC

KAMCHATKA

Yakutsk

Lena River

SEA OF OKHOTSK

SAKHALIN

Yenisei River

Irkutsk

MONGOLIA

MANCHURIA

Vladivostok

SEA OF JAPAN

JAPAN

YELLOW SEA

1 Early Years

THE Soviet Union—commonly called Russia—is the largest country in the world. Its land area of 8.6 million square miles comprises one-sixth of the land area of the earth. It is twice the size of the world's second largest country, China, and almost two and one-half times larger than the United States, including all of its territories and possessions. It stretches for 6,000 miles from Europe to the Aleutians and 3,000 miles from the Arctic north to the hot wastelands of Central Asia. The country is so huge that when night is falling in the western area, day is breaking in the eastern regions. In the Bering Strait, the Soviet Union is seven miles from Alaska, and yet its southern border is only nine miles from India. It is a direct neighbor of a half-dozen Western European countries as well as of Afghanistan, Iran, Turkey, and China.

Almost all of European Russia lies above the 46th parallel, which is approximately the latitude that separates the United

States and Canada. The climate in this area is one of extremes—short, hot summers and long, very cold winters. Thus, the agricultural growing season is relatively short, even in the southern areas. Further, dry spells are not uncommon, with resulting crop failures.

The Union of Soviet Socialist Republics (USSR)—the full name of the Soviet Union—has approximately 230 million people. Three-quarters of them are Slavs, and the other quarter are scattered among more than sixty different nationalities. Except for high mountains in Asia, and the Ural Mountains that divide European and Asiatic Russia, the land is flat. Vast plains, known as the steppes, and endless forests are predominant physical features of the land.

This giant of nations was not always so huge nor was it always a nation. A thousand years ago, Eastern Slavic tribes, the ancestors of the Russian people, settled along the Dnieper River. Within a short time, they spread until they had settled as far north as Lake Ladoga and from the banks of the Western Dvina River to the Oka and Upper Voïga rivers. They established autonomous city-states, one of the earliest and strongest of which was Kiev. Other strong city-states were Great Novgorod and Smolensk. In the twelfth century, Moscow was founded. By the beginning of the fourteenth century, it had become the center of a loose federation of a number of city-states and the home of a long line of Russian rulers.

In the early thirteenth century, the Tatars, under Genghis Khan and his successors, conquered Russia. After more than two hundred years of Tatar rule, Russia overthrew her Asiatic conquerors in the middle of the fifteenth century. Under Ivan the Great (1462–1505), Vasili III (1505–1533), and Ivan the Terrible (1547–1584), Russia was unified and strengthened. Beginning with Ivan the Terrible, Russia expanded to Siberia, and subsequent rulers, such as Peter the Great (1682–1725), and Catherine II (1762–1796), further expanded the territory of Russia to the Baltic Sea on the west and to the Pacific Ocean on the east.

From about the first millennium after Christ and lasting until the early eighteenth century, slavery was not uncommon. Most of the slaves were an inheritance from the period of nomad raids, Tatar conquest, and Russian expansion. The slave was the chattel of his owner, had no rights, and paid no taxes. He was at the complete mercy of his master who could sell him as property or, if he wished, even kill him. The master was legally responsible for all actions of his slave. Slavery did not come to an end until serfdom was fully established during the reign of Peter the Great.

Serfdom in Russia had a long and complex history. As early as the eleventh and twelfth centuries, the agricultural worker, or peasant, owned his own dwelling, tools, and animals and had a good deal of social and economic freedom. He was known by the name of *smerd*, which philologists believe comes from an ancient root meaning "man," but is associated with the Russian verb *smerdeti*, meaning to have a bad smell. The peasant was free to buy and sell his property, if he had any, and he was free from bondage. If he lacked seed, animals, and tools, he made arrangements to till a landlord's land in return for these necessities.

During ensuing centuries, the peasant made an arrangement, like a sharecropper, to share his crops with the landlord in return for tools, land, seed, and animals. The share varied, but was usually half of the crops to the landlord and half to himself. He often became indebted to the landlord and obligated himself to pay off his debt by working for him. This often amounted to one day's work each week. In other cases, he made an arrangement to use the landlord's land and to pay an *obrok*, or quitrent. This was a definite amount of the crop or a definite amount of labor. At the end of a harvest, he would enter into another arrangement with the landlord or, if his debt were paid, he could leave if he wanted to. By the time of the first *sudebnik*, or legal code, of Ivan III in 1497, the period in which he could leave was set on the festival of St. George in the autumn of the year.

By the beginning of the sixteenth century, after the Tatars had been defeated, land became available in Siberia and elsewhere, and the number of peasants leaving the landlord's land increased. Many landlords suffered a labor shortage and exerted pressure on the government to limit free movement by the peasants. In order to protect the landowners, the czar, Boris Godunov, promulgated a law in 1597 by which the peasant was bound to the soil in certain ways although he could still exercise his right of removal during the period of the festival of St. George. In 1649, a new code of law firmly fixed the peasant to the land by increasing the landlord's lawful authority over him; bondage now became not only an economic fact but a legal one as well.

By the eighteenth century, the slaves, the sharecroppers, and the free agricultural workers had become merged into one large grouping, the serfs, who were regarded as the property of the landed proprietors or of the state. However, it must be made clear that although all serfs were peasants, a large number of the peasants were not serfs in the sense that they were tied to the land and performed only agricultural labor. There were crown peasants, who were under a special jurisdiction and could move about freely as long as they paid a modest passport fee. There were house serfs, who worked as domestics on the master's estate; and there were serfs who were trained as actors, musicians, and handymen. Serfs worked in their master's industrial enterprises, and other serfs, often in association with their masters, engaged in commerce. Some serfs became well off, and a few even became rich. Nevertheless, the overwhelming majority of peasants and almost all of the serfs were desperately poor.

In 1797 William Richardson, an Englishman who spent several years in Russia in the latter part of the eighteenth century, described the peasants as follows:

> The peasants [i.e., serfs] in Russia . . . are in a state of abject slavery; and are reckoned the property of the nobles to whom they belong, as much as their dogs and horses. Indeed, the wealth of a great man in Russia is not computed by the extent of land he possesses, or by the quantity of grain he can bring to market, but by the number of his slaves. . . . The owner has the power of selling his slave, or of hiring his labour to other persons.

Richardson insisted on referring to the serfs as "slaves," and in many respects they were, indeed, comparable to a chattel slave. Over the years, the state more and more allowed the relationship between serf and master to be controlled by the master. As a result, the serf owners became virtual masters over the serfs, and the latter were deprived of almost all state protection.

Serfs were counted as capital, the same as land, buildings, and other immovable property. Like the land itself, the serfs were bought, sold, and given as presents by the hundreds and even by the thousands at a time. In many cases, the serfs were disposed of as family groups as well as individually. Virtually helpless in face of the discriminatory laws against him, the serf was unable to cope with the almost unlimited power of his masters. When he complained on occasion, he was punished for his insubordination by a whipping with the knout or by exile to the icy wastes of Siberia.

The czars were great givers of gifts to their favorites. Often, the gift was in the form of land, at other times in the form of serfs. Peter the Great was a most generous dispenser of favors; he gave away tens of thousands of serfs. The czars that followed were even more generous, and in the years between 1740 and 1800, more than 1,300,000 male serfs with their wives and children were handed over to court favorites. Catherine the Great is said to have given away more than 800,000 serfs. On special occasions such as birthdays, weddings, and birth of heirs to the throne, thousands of acres of land and thousands of serfs of both sexes were distributed.

2 The Village

THROUGHOUT Russia, whether in the distant north or the southern steppes, the village dominated the national life. Although details differed—huts made of clay in southern Russia and of logs in the north—the day-to-day life and the appearance of the village remained virtually unchanged for hundreds of years.

Usually villages were laid out with the houses in one or more lines along the banks of a river or a lake. In larger villages, there were several lines of houses, running either parallel or perpendicular to one another. The houses were spaced a small distance from each other to prevent the spread of fire from one house to another. The size of the villages varied from hamlets that had a few houses to villages having as many as five hundred households. Most of the large villages were in the south while those of the north tended to be small in size.

The houses, barns, and sheds clustered along a village street were usually built of unpainted logs. The narrow, unpaved streets were muddy in the spring and winter, and dusty in the summer. Occasionally a vegetable garden would be planted near a house, but usually open fields beyond the settlement were staked off for sowing and there was a common pasture for the animals of the village.

The appearance of the villages was drab. The hewn-log houses were covered by thatched roofs that became blackened by the elements. There were few trees and no flowers. The *izba,* or hut, usually faced the street, and behind it was a large courtyard, strewn with mounds of straw and wood. Here the family spent a good deal of its time, and here, too, the animals were quartered when they were not out to pasture.

As many as twenty persons sometimes shared the izba, a one- or two-room building that was rarely more than a square fifteen to twenty feet in length and width. The *pech,* or stove, dominated

A peasant village in prerevolutionary Russia.

Novosti from Sovfoto

The interior of a peasant hut.

the room, taking up as much as one-fourth of the area. These stoves were used for heating the room as well as for cooking. Some of the more prosperous peasants had a stove with a chimney, but the poorer ones did not: the smoke was supposed to escape by a hole in the wall or through the door. When these methods failed, which was often the case, the smoke hung in the room, blackening the walls.

The combination of odors from animals, humans, cooking, and stale air was overwhelming. A character in one of Ivan Turgenev's short stories rationalized this odor by saying that it was "necessary for a cottage to smell of life." However, a young Russian nobleman, Paul von Birukoff, who devoted himself to uplifting the peasants, described his experience upon first visiting a peasant hut in the 1890s as one in which he felt "as if my body, unaccustomed to this polluted, suffocating atmosphere, was poisoned."

Of his visit to a peasant household, he wrote:

> Stooping down, I creep through the low door, and enter the hut. A damp and suffocating air meets me, so that I am near fainting. A few rays of light struggle with difficulty through a small window, for which an opening has been dug through the snow. A woman is at the oven, busy with a stone jar in her hand. Behind her, two little children, covered with rags and pale and dirty, are sitting on a bench, sucking a hard crust. In another corner, something covered with a battered sheepskin cloak is lying on a bench.

The interior of the hut had no furniture in the conventional sense. There was, perhaps, a large, unpolished table and a few long wooden shelves about two feet deep, running along the walls. These were used for sitting during the day and for sleeping at night. At bedtime, some members climbed onto the upper tier of these shelves, which Stepniak, a peasant reformer in the late nineteenth century, described as "running all along the upper part of the wall, like hammocks in the ship's cabin." There were no mattresses of any kind. Sometimes there were a few rags spread on the benches. Writes Stepniak: "The everyday coat, just taken off, serves as a blanket. Beds are a luxury hardly known, and very little appreciated by the Russian *muzhiks* [peasants]. . . . In the winter, the large top of the stone oven is the favorite sleeping place, and generally reserved for the elders, so that they may keep their old bones warm."

The Frenchman Chantreau, who visited Russia in the late eighteenth century, noted that all the inhabitants of the hut "slept with their clothes on. The family lie on benches, on the ground, or more readily on the stove. . . . Often the men, women, and children sleep all together, without any regard to sex or condition. In some cottages, we perceived a sort of frame, six or seven feet high, which they shift at pleasure from one end of the room to the other. In the center of this, there are several planks fixed horizontally above one another. Here, the family sleeps, often with their feet and head hanging; a posture very straining for strangers not accustomed to this kind of bed."

No peasant hut was without its icons or religious paintings, which often were placed in one corner of the room. It was in this icon corner, incidentally, that guests were entertained. Traditionally, this corner was diagonally opposite the stove. In some peasant huts, there were suspended from the ceiling in the middle of the room a vessel full of holy water and a lamp, which was lit only on special occasions. The lamp faintly illumined the icon or crudely painted house saint.

As late as the middle of the nineteenth century, a visitor from the West noted that "taken as a whole, Russia is just one vast village." In all of Russia in the year 1856, there were only ten cities with over 50,000 people. Of the 678 centers officially termed cities, 611 contained less than 15,000 persons.

This situation remained essentially the same until well after the Russian revolution—most of the people living in villages that dotted the countryside in a monotonous similarity.

3 The Mir

IN old Russia, the peasant communities had a unique organizational structure, which differed widely from the peasant or farming communities in other European countries. This was the institution known as the *mir*, the *obschina*, or commune. The size of the mir varied greatly, from as few as twenty or thirty *dvors*, or households, to many hundreds. A dvor consisted of one or several houses, with one or more married couples and their children in each.

The three main "authority" units of the mir were the *khozain*, the head of the household; the *starosta*, the village elder; and the village assembly composed of the heads of the households. The khozain was the ruling male of the household and had authority over it. The starosta was elected by the khozains of the mir and acted as a kind of arbitrator or referee.

The mir governed the life of the peasant and that of the community. It specified how much land was available for him to cultivate, what crops he should plant, and when he should harvest them. It assessed his obligations and acted as the guardian of his rights. Its most important function—and one that most vitally affected the peasant—was its role in redividing the land.

All members of the mir had a right to an allotment of land for cultivation separately by the individual peasant household. The household also had hereditary possession of its hut and garden. The pasture land—and sometimes the meadows and forests—was held in common, with no individual peasant household actually owning the land. Each household tilled its own parcel of land, which was periodically allocated by the mir. In brief, the rights to the land were held in common, but the possession or cultivation of the land was individual.

The frequency of land reallocation varied from area to area, and even from mir to mir. It could be done every ten years, every six years or, in a few cases, as often as every year. The peasant worked the land until the next allocation, when the land was again redistributed. The amount the household would get on re-allocation would depend upon changes in a household—births, deaths, marriages, illnesses. The main factor, however, that decided the amount of land each household would receive, was the number of taxable persons in it.

Tax assessment and collection were the responsibility of the mir itself. All members of the mir were held jointly liable by the czarist government for the payment of taxes. If a household did not pay its taxes, the mir had the right and the power to hire out a member of the defaulting household. It could even remove the head of the household and, in his place, appoint another member of the household to be its head.

All earnings by the household from any source were supposed to go into a common pool. This applied even to peasants who had left their village and were working in the cities or elsewhere. This procedure was enforced by the mir's jurisdiction over the issuance of a permit to qualify for a government passport. A passport was essential if a peasant wished to leave his native village.

There were many cases in which the male head of the household was ill, had died, or had left the mir to seek work in a city.

Often, if there was an older male in the household, he would represent the household. In some cases, the wife would do so. Depending upon the character and wit of the woman, she would have a greater or lesser weight at the assembly. However, in general, the woman was more tolerated than respected because of the then-prevailing Russian view that women were inferior to men.

Almost all actions of the peasant households had a relation to the work of the commune as a whole and thus had to have the approval of the assembly. As a result, the members of the mir were closely tied to each other and intimately bound not only in their work but also in their social life. It is almost safe to say that the business of one was the business of all and the affairs of all were the concern of each. For example, the allocation of the strips of land for each household was determined by the mir upon the basis of those who were adult and able-bodied. This decision affected the other members of the mir with regard to the disposition of the strips of land, since some strips were more desirable than others. Furthermore, since the payment of taxes to the imperial treasury was the collective obligation of the mir, the contribution of each household to the general tax fund was of vital importance to all. This was so, even though the general tax levy on the mir was determined on the basis of the total number of taxable persons in each household.

One of the most interesting as well as unique aspects of the mir was the functioning of the village assembly. These assemblies were called periodically, usually on a Saturday or Sunday. In most cases, they were held out of doors, since few villages had a house large enough to accommodate all the mir members.

A typical assembly was one in which the entire population of the mir gathered in a meadow. It was very casual, with groups of the peasants conversing among themselves, as though they were at a picnic or outing. Children played at their games and the young men engaged in horseplay, sang, or teased the girls. Eventually, with no particular signal being given, the meeting began.

There were few rules of order. Persons spoke up when they felt like it, often several at the same time. The discussion frequently became a confused mixture of unintelligible voices. Tempers would flair; curses would be shouted. It appeared that some disputants would come to blows, but they very rarely did. The loud talk, the curses, the tempers, so it seemed, were part of the spirit of the assembly. Then, as though by some prearranged signal, some kind of order was established and the affairs of the day would come up for discussion. Voices would be raised for or against the issue. The starosta, who acted more as a mediator than a chairman, would put in a word or two. It was his privilege to call an unruly peasant to order or to chastise him for a foolish or inflammatory remark. When the assembled peasants appeared to have talked themselves out on the matter at hand, the starosta, sensing the prevailing opinion of the assembly, would bring the matter to a close. As one observer noted, he might say, "Well, orthodox, have you decided so?" and the crowd would probably shout *"Ladno! Ladno!"* that is to say, "Agreed! Agreed!"

Usually things were settled by unanimous consent. On the rare occasion when there was a definite division of opinion, the starosta might ask those who were in favor of the issue to step to one side and those who were against to step to the other. The majority opinion prevailed. There was no appeal from the mir's decision—it was final.

Some of the matters that might come up for a decision were the following: when to begin plowing; what action should be taken against persons who did not pay their taxes; the admission of a new member into the commune; the construction of a building; and, most important, the division and allocation of the communal land.

The starosta was not necessarily either the oldest or the wisest in the mir. It might be supposed that this position of prestige would be sought after by a head of a household. Usually, this was not the case. He viewed the office not as a sign of respect by the community but as a job that was both burdensome and unrewarding. The bronze medal around his neck marking his office and the few rubles he received he viewed as small reward for the trouble and time. The office of starosta was usually filled not by, as might be assumed, an eager office seeker but by either default or community pressure. As an eyewitness in nineteenth-century

Russia to one such election of a starosta, the historian D. Mackenzie Wallace wrote:

> "Whom shall we choose [for starosta]?"
>
> As soon as this question is asked, several peasants look down to the
> ground or try in some other way to avoid attracting attention, lest their
> names should be suggested. When the silence has continued a minute
> or two, the graybeard says, "There is Alexei Ivanoff; he has not served
> yet!"
>
> "Yes, yes, Alexei Ivanoff." shout half a dozen voices, belonging
> probably to peasants who fear they may be elected.
>
> Alexei protests in the strongest terms. He cannot say that he is ill,
> because his big ruddy face would give him the lie direct, but he finds
> half a dozen other reasons why he should not be chosen, and accord-
> ingly requests to be excused. But his protestations are not listened to,
> and the proceedings terminate. A new village elder has been duly
> elected.

The origin of the unique Russian institution known as the mir
has long been a controversial subject among scholars. Some historians trace the mir back to the breakup of the tribal form of organization among the Eastern Slavs long before the beginning of
the second millennium. Little is known, but the clans were
thought to have broken down into large family units, headed by a
patriarch, which had many characteristics of the commune.

Other historians dispute this idea that the rural commune developed from the tribal societies that existed in early Russia. The
Russian historian B. N. Chicherin, for example, believed that the
village communes came into existence as late as the sixteenth century as a direct result of new government regulations that bound
the peasants to their place of residence as a tax measure. He
argued further that the principle of periodically redistributing the
land among the members of the mir was not, as some persons
claimed, an equalizing socialistic measure, but a practical way to
meet the government's capitation tax, instituted during the regime
of Peter I.

There were some observers who took an idealistic view of the
communes. For instance, the German scholar Baron Haxthausen,
who wrote one of the first accounts of the workings of the mir, believed they were free republics, and that the only limitation to

their freedom was in their payment of a fixed rent to the lord. He noted that the rural commune of Russia was without precedent in Europe.

The Slavophiles, members of a nineteenth-century movement that emphasized the national individuality of Russia and opposed Westernization, believed that the communal principle was at the base of Russia's historical development from the dawn of its history to modern times. They insisted that the mir had its origins in the tribal organization of the early Slavs. On the other hand, those persons who believed in the Westernization of Russia, viewed the mir as mainly the product of government practices and decrees.

The question of the origin and development of the mir was of more than scholarly interest. From the middle of the nineteenth century on, when the question of abolishing serfdom was a burning question, the entire problem of the relationship of peasant, lord, and government became paramount. Violent arguments arose whether the rural commune was a definite sign of Russian backwardness and a break with progress or whether the commune was uniquely Russian and could lead the Russian agricultural population toward a better way of life. In the years after the emancipation of the serfs in 1863, the land-equalizing communes were even referred to as examples of "popular democracy in action."

Astute observers of the old Russian scene such as D. Mackenzie Wallace called the village communes "capital specimens of representative Constitutional government of the extreme democratic type. . . . As to its thoroughly democratic character there can be no possible doubt. The Elder represents merely the executive power. All the real authority resides in the Assembly, of which all Heads of Households are members."

Except for occasional observers of rural Russia, usually foreigners, the communes were ignored as a social, economic, and political organizational phenomenon until the nineteenth century. Then, as pressure increased for an end to serfdom, the communes attracted active political interest as well as scholarly inspection. Not only were they analyzed, defended, or attacked by the Slavophiles and the Westernizers, as has been mentioned, but they became drawn into the ever-increasing radicalization of Russian affairs themselves. Various political groups had their views on the peasant question. And the peasant question itself was inextricably tied to the existence, functioning, and future of the mir.

The mir was scrutinized; it was idealized. It had friends and enemies in all political camps from extreme conservatives to extreme radicals.

Some persons and groups glorified the mir as efficient, egalitarian, and democratic. It was viewed as a unique ancient Russian organization with deep roots in the habits, customs, and character of the Russian people. It was considered to be an exemplary organization with respect to self-government. The Slavophile Stepniak wrote:

"The peasants have applied their collective intelligence not to material questions alone, nor within the domain apportioned to them by law. The mir recognizes no restraint on its autonomy. In the opinion of the peasants themselves, the mir's authority embraces, indeed, all domains and branches of peasant life. Unless the police and the local officers are at hand to prevent what is considered an abuse of power, the peasant's mir is always likely to exceed its authority."

The very word "mir" seemed to signify something that was venerable or even holy. In the minds of some it signified, too, not only the commune itself but the very universe. An almost endless list of proverbs, nearly all laudatory and proud, points up this view. Here are only a few sayings about the mir that were common in old Russia:

God alone is judge of the mir.
Throw all upon the mir, it will bear all.
All that the mir decides must be done.
The mir is great . . . it is a surging billow.
The neck and shoulders of the mir are broad.
The mir sighs, and the rock is rent asunder.
The mir sobs, and it re-echoes in the forest.
A thread of the mir becomes a shirt for the naked.
No one in the world can separate from the mir.

The critics of the mir insisted that the village communes were not only harmful to the peasants but slowed the progress of Russia itself. Some persons insisted that there was little that was idyllic about the communes. They were, they said, cesspools of poverty, filth, and ignorance. The "town meeting" or democratic quality of the assembly was no more, they insisted, than shouting matches that usually degenerated into drunken brawls.

Even Stepniak himself would not give the communes unqualified praise. Although he defended them as unique Russian institutions, he condemned them, too:

> The mir [he wrote] is generally composed of a mass of beggars, who cannot afford the assistance they would otherwise give, and of a few *kulaks* and mir-eaters, who sell their help at a low price. . . . The modern mir is completely subject to the local police and the administration which allows it the free exercise of its powers of self-government only when there is no inducement for officials to interfere. . . . The abuse of authority on the part of inferior police agents and administrators, and their cruel treatment of the helpless peasantry, form one of the most sickening and bloody chapters in the annals of Russian aristocracy.

Although there was—and is—a sharp difference of opinion on the mir as a desirable social relationship of people in a rural setting, there was one area, however, in which there seemed little doubt that the mir was a brake upon progress; this was in the economic area. The mir, by its very nature, prevented the introduction and development of agricultural policies that would have taken advantage of new technologies to increase output and thus improve the peasants' lives. In a sense, the authority of the mir and the rigidity of its structure severely limited the adjustment the peasant himself could make to his own condition of life.

While in various countries some progress in agriculture was being made, say, during the nineteenth and early twentieth centuries, there was little if any progress in this regard in Russia. The agricultural output, and thus the lives of the peasants, changed little over the years and rarely for the better. For those peasants who dreamed of a better life, the time-dulled workings of the mir seemed to offer little hope that these agricultural communes were the solution to their misery, poverty, and oppression. If change was to come to Russia, it would not come because of the so-called democratic makeup of the mir but, as it developed, despite it.

4 The Landowner

UNLIKE the nobility in European countries, the Russian nobles measured their wealth not by the amount of land they had but by the number of male serfs, or souls, they owned. A landlord who owned a thousand serfs was considered extremely wealthy. Ownership of five hundred to one thousand made him a proprietor of great means. He was moderately wealthy if he owned from one hundred to five hundred; a petty noble might own as few as twenty-five. Usually, if he had fewer than twenty-five souls he was considered poor.

In the nineteenth century, some landlords had thousands of serfs. For example, Count D. N. Sheremetev owned almost 300,000 serfs of both sexes, Count Vorontsov had more than 37,000 male serfs, and Prince Iusupov owned 33,000 male serfs. These extremely wealthy lords, however, were a tiny fraction of the serf-owning nobility. According to the census of 1858, 40 percent of all landlords owned from 1 to 20 souls; 34 percent owned from

A Landlord Exchanges Peasants for Dogs.
Painting by Tara Shevchenko (1814–1861).

21 to 100 souls, 19 percent owned from 101 to 500 souls; 2 percent owned from 500 to 1,000 souls; and 1 percent owned over 1,000 souls. However, of great significance is the fact that there was a concentration of serf ownership in the hands of a relatively few powerful landowners; 3 percent of the largest landowners—those owning more than 500 souls—accounted for the ownership of 44 percent of all male serfs. The landowners who owned only 1 to 20 serfs, who constituted 40 percent of all landowners, owned only 3 percent of male serfs. Eight souls was the average number of serfs for each landlord. A number of nobles were so impoverished that they owned no serfs.

This unequal distribution of ownership of serfs made wide divisions among the nobility. A prince in old Russia could be a man who owned tens of thousands of acres of land and thousands of serfs or he could be so impoverished that he literally had to beg for his food, clothing, and lodging. For instance, in 1771 a group of nobles told the Russian senate that more than two hundred young nobles in their jurisdiction wished to join the imperial service, but did not have the clothing to wear so that they could report for duty. Some nobles were so poor that they tilled a bit of land like any peasant and, in fact, led almost peasant-like lives. It was reported that in Riazan one-fourth of noble families were so poor that "together with their peasants they form one family, eat at one table, and live in one hut."

There were many reasons for the poverty of so many nobles. One of the most important causes was the centuries-old custom of dividing up a lord's inheritance among his survivors—sons, daughters, and wife. This practice lessened the wealth of each to such a degree that, in time, they and their descendants were reduced to owning very small parcels of land and few, if any, serfs. There were wealthy families that in only three generations had so divided up the inheritance that all the descendants were poverty-stricken. Quite often, descendants of a particularly prolific member of a family were at the poverty level while descendants of a not-so-prolific member were wealthy.

The wide variation of wealth among the nobility resulted in a wide variation of life styles. The wealthy lord, whether he made his home in the city or the country, often lived in the style of an Eastern potentate. The poor lord, again whether he resided in the country or city, often lived no better than the city worker or the peasant. The poor prince scrounging for a few rubles in Moscow or St. Petersburg (now Leningrad) and the poverty-stricken noble dying of boredom and beset by debts in some isolated country setting are familiar characters in Russian novels and plays.

The life style of the lord, however, was not completely dependent on his economic situation. Whether they were rich or poor, most members of the nobility had a distinctly different way about them than other members of Russian society. Generally, they were educated; interested in the arts, especially the theater; looked toward Europe, especially France, for cultural and social patterns; and had little affinity for the so-called Protestant ethic of work, thrift, and sobriety.

These were not always the dominant characteristics of the nobility. Over the years, their outlook and actions had changed significantly.

In early Russian history, the noble had been a warrior who lived a rugged life both on his estate and on the battlefield. Strength, courage, loyalty, and the ability to bear great hardship were virtues to which he aspired. As a warrior-prince, he shared the hardships of battle with his ordinary soldiers and lived a hazardous life. For example, Prince Vladimir Monomakh, who ruled in Kiev in the early part of the twelfth century, left a testament to his sons, written shortly before his death. After recounting his own exploits and dozens of virtues that an honest ruler and human being should be guided by, he proudly noted:

> In war and at the hunt, by night and by day, in heat and in cold, I did whatever my servant had to do, and gave myself no rest. Without relying on lieutenants or messengers, I did whatever was necessary; I looked to every disposition in my household. At the hunt, I posted the hunters, and I looked after the stable, the falcons, and the hawks. I did not allow the mighty to distress the common peasant or the poverty-stricken widow. . . . Without fear of death, of war, or of wild beasts, do a man's work, my sons, as God sets it before you.

Over the centuries, this warrior-prince type of noble disappeared. By the time of Peter the Great in the early eighteenth century, the ideal type of noble was a man who was skilled in, say, fortifications, engineering, government administration, or any profession in which he could perform meritorious service to the state. However, Peter's plan to bring the nobility into serious work on behalf of the crown lasted only a brief while after his death. Except for a small number of nobles who made their careers in government or the army, most nobles by the time of Catherine the Great in the late eighteenth century had been relieved of any requirements of service to the crown. The majority of them, whether rich or poor, led lives in which employment, either political or economic, was not a part of the pattern of their lives.

They lived in idleness and spent their lives looking for pleasures or diversions. The nobleman-turned-fop paralleled in many ways the fops of the time in Western Europe. Others, many of whom insisted on speaking French instead of Russian, posed as men of letters or philosophers. The Russian historian Vasili Kluchevsky wrote of them:

This philosopher-nobleman was the typical representative of that social class whose task it was to carry Russian society forward along the road of progress; hence it is necessary to point out his chief characteristics. His social position was founded upon political injustice and crowned with idleness. From the hands of his teacher, the cantor and clerk of the village church, he passed into the control of a French tutor, rounded off his education in Italian theatres or French restaurants, made use of his acquirements in the drawing-rooms of St. Petersburg and finished his days in a private study in Moscow, or at some country place, with a volume of Voltaire in his hands. On Povarskaia [a fashionable avenue in old Moscow] or in the country in Tula *gubernia* [province], with his volume of Voltaire in his hands, he was a strange phenomenon. All his adopted manners, customs, tastes, sympathies, his language itself—all were foreign, imported. He had no organic connections with his surroundings, no sort of serious business in life. A foreigner among his own people, he tried to make himself at home among foreigners. In European society, he was a kind of adopted child. In Europe he was looked upon, indeed, as a re-costumed Tatar, and at home, people saw in him a Frenchman born in Russia.

This type of nobleman was most in evidence in such large cities as St. Petersburg or Moscow and among those who had some connection with the court. In the more rural areas, the nobles made a pathetic and sometimes futile effort to ape their city cousins. Still, the provincial noble was closer in his tastes and life style to the prevailing life style of the urban Europeanized Russian noble than he was to the Russian common man—the peasant.

In the economic field, the noble's lack of interest in new agricultural techniques doomed the peasants under his jurisdiction to a life in which there was no hope of escaping from poverty and back-breaking toil. In many cases, it also doomed the landlord himself to declining income as a result of low crop yields and unprofitable agricultural and marketing methods.

In the novels and plays of such writers as Nikolai Gogol, Ivan Turgenev, and Anton Chekhov, the provincial nobleman-landlord is a favorite Russian character. Often he is depicted as a somewhat lost soul, whose basic characteristic seems to be one of subtle fatalism. An early twentieth-century observer of Russian life, Harold Williams, noted that among the country gentry "there are endless difficulties, but it seems to the proprietors incredible that they should be insurmountable. A way out is sure to be found, things cannot be as bad as they appear. Someone is sure to help, either the Government or the elements or some vague, friendly Providence. Indeed the gentry are just as responsible as the peasantry for the prevalence in Russian conversation of such comfortable optimistic phrases as *Obrazuiestsia* (It will come out all right)...."

It was to this class that, over the centuries, the power had been given to guide the lives of Russia's millions of peasants, who made up some 90 percent of the country's population prior to the Revolution of 1917. As far as the peasants were concerned, the government reigned but the landlords ruled. By the eighteenth century, the nobles had established their sole right to own land and serfs. Previously, other groups such as merchants and, especially, the church had the right to own serfs. In fact, until Catherine the Great's reign, the church was one of the largest owners of serfs. In 1747, for instance, in Great Russia and Siberia alone, the church owned more than 900,000 male serfs. All this came to an end in 1764 when Catherine confiscated ecclesiastical property and converted the church peasants into state peasants.

The nobles now had clear social, cultural, and economic advantages over other classes in Russian society. This position was maintained through the crown's method of tax legislation, which was directed at the peasantry who were under the jurisdiction of the nobles.

The buying and selling of serfs by the nobles was a key element in the economy as it affected and was affected by the noble-serf relationship. The serf owners borrowed money from special governmental credit bureaus that had been established to aid the nobles and used their serfs as collateral.

The price of serfs varied, depending upon the job required of the serf or his skills. Generally, those used for domestic service were less expensive than those who were tied to a land purchase. Although most serfs were unskilled and uneducated, there were some who had either high skills, some education, or both.

For example, Prince Potemkin is said to have paid forty thousand rubles to Field Marshal Razumovski for a fifty-piece serf orchestra. A talented serf actress was reputed to have been sold for five thousand rubles. Depending upon the demand at the time, the price of serfs varied from as low as three rubles for a male to as high as two hundred rubles—except for serfs with special accomplishments.

The traffic in girl serfs was heavy. The price paid for an especially attractive young female serf could run as high as five hundred rubles. Generally, the price was around fifty rubles for an ordinary housemaid. The purchasing of young female serfs was widespread, and many nobles simply purchased a girl serf who attracted him and sold her when she no longer appealed to him. It was a practice that was engaged in by almost all of the wealthier class and even by those who expressed themselves against the condition of serfdom. For instance, the novelist Ivan Turgenev, who was opposed to serfdom and wrote many stories on the cruelty and oppression of the system, paid his cousin seven hundred rubles for a pretty serf girl with whom he entertained himself during his exile to his estate in 1852.

There were cases in which landed gentry would allow their girl serfs to go to the cities to become prostitutes and then collect from one hundred to two hundred rubles yearly from them. The town of Ivanovo, a texile center, was one of the centers for the girl serf market, and buyers came from many parts of Russia to purchase them. Although the government several times passed decrees to forbid or limit the traffic in girl serfs, in practice this trade was never completely stopped and was engaged in by merchants and others as well as by the nobility.

In addition to allowing the landowners to buy and sell serfs, the government allowed the landowners more and more judicial and police power over them. Until the eighteenth century, there were a number of restrictive laws on the power of the landowners over the serfs. But all through the eighteenth century one law after another was struck down, so that by the end of the century, the owner of a serf had virtually every kind of power over him, except the power of putting him to death. Even in this regard, however, despite the law, the noble had actual power to put a serf to death. The lord could not have him executed, but he had the right to flog a serf as hard as he pleased. To accomplish this, the lord could use a wide variety of flogging instruments—rods, staffs, whips, bundles of leather thongs twisted with wire. And if the flogging resulted in death, the landowner was rarely punished. The most extreme punishment the lord could legally hand out was banishment of the serf to Siberia. As early as the sixteenth century, this was encouraged by the government as a means of settling this vastly underpopulated area.

The life of a serf was considered cheap and expendable. For example, the Englishman William Richardson wrote that "sometimes a boyar [lord] shall give his slave to a neighboring boyar in exchange for a dog or a horse. The owner may inflict on his slaves whatever punishment he pleases, and for any offense. It is against the law, indeed, to put any of them to death; yet it happens, sometimes, that a poor slave dies of wounds he receives from a passionate and unrelenting superior."

Whether a serf was treated well or cruelly depended almost entirely on the nature of his master. As the book *The Antidote*, published in French in 1768, pointed out, the "good or bad treatment of domestic servants depends much more on the good or bad morality of the masters than on the laws of the country."

The history and literature of the master-serf relationship in Russia are full of examples and stories of unbridled cruelty of the master to his serf. For example, in one year on the Borisovo estate of Prince Radziwill, his agents beat to death forty-four serfs, blinded forty-two, and otherwise mutilated thirteen. Sadistic masters had almost complete license to practice their sadism on their serfs. One of the most publicized instances is the case of Daria Saltykov, who inherited six hundred serfs from her husband in 1756. Within seven years, she had tortured, mutilated, or whipped to death scores of peasants. The crimes were so shocking that this was one instance where a master was punished. After a six-year investigation, she was stripped of her noble rank, pilloried for one hour in Moscow, and banished for life to a convent.

The reaction of the government in the Saltykov case was unusual. Usually, the masters were not punished. During Catherine the Great's reign, which lasted for thirty-four years, only six landowners were known to have been punished for crimes against their serfs. In fact, the Great Catherine, after a tour in which she was annoyed by the number of peasant petitions against their masters, issued an edict in 1767, in which it was decreed a criminal act for a serf to petition against his master. The punishment was a beating with the knout or exile to Siberia.

Some years later, a Frenchman who had lived in Russia for many years wrote that the domination of the Russian master over his serfs was greater than any sovereign had over his subjects. Catherine herself gave royal confirmation of this viewpoint in a letter to the French encylopedist Diderot in which she said the Russian serf owners were "free to do in their estates whatever seemed best to them, except to give the death penalty, which is prohibited to them."

The reaction of the peasants to their masters' oppression varied. In a few instances, they struck back by burning the master's property and even revolted on a broad scale such as during the Razin and Pugachev insurrections, which took place in the seventeenth and eighteenth centuries respectively. However, in general, they submitted because of lethargy, fear, or custom. The British historian D. MacKenzie Wallace, for example, who traveled through a good part of European Russia in the 1870s, gives this anecdote about the manner in which peasants approached their master and his reaction to them:

In the evening it often happens that a little group of peasants come into the court, and ask to see the "master." The master goes to the door, and generally finds that they have some favor to request. In reply to his question, "Well, children, what do you want?" they tell their story in a confused, rambling way, several of them speaking at a time. He has to question and cross-question them before he comes to understand clearly what they desire. If he tells them he cannot grant it, they probably do not accept a first refusal, but endeavor by means of supplication to make him reconsider his decision. Stepping forward a little, and bowing low, one of the group begins in a half-respectful, half-familiar, caressing tone—"Little father, Ivan Ivan'itch, be gracious; you are our father, and we are your children"—and so on. Ivan Ivan'itch good-naturedly listens, and again explains that he cannot grant what they ask. But they have still hopes of gaining their point by entreaty, and continue their supplications till at last his patience is exhausted and he says to them in a paternal tone, "Now, enough!

enough! you are blockheads—blockheads all round! There's no use talking, it can't be done." And with these words he enters the house so as to prevent all further discussion.

Ivan Turgenev was a master in describing the lord-peasant relationship. In one story, a serf is beaten by his master, and when he is asked why he was chastised, he replies: "It was for a reason, sir, for a reason. At our place they don't punish for trifles: that's not the custom with us. No, no. Our gentleman is not that sort: our gentleman . . . you won't find such a one in the whole province."

In every society in every country and in every era in which there have been master and slave, the "good" and the "bad" master are to be found. In the literature of all societies—whether an *Uncle Tom's Cabin* in the United States or a *Sportsman's Sketches* or a *Dead Souls* in Russia—these variations are highlighted. Whether the Russian lord was more cruel than, say, the Southern slaveowner in pre-Civil War United States is a debatable question. Certainly, there were those of the nobility who abhorred the system of serfdom and there were those who passionately defended it.

In practice, there were masters who gave the peasants of the commune a great deal of liberty in running their own affairs as long as they gave him the agreed-upon goods and a certain number of days' work. There were other lords who involved themselves fully in the affairs of their serfs and ruled them with an iron fist. There were some owners who managed their own estates and personally tried to squeeze every bit of profit from their lands and their serfs. Owners who were retired army officers established a firm, almost military, discipline over their serfs. And there were absentee landowners, who lived in cities that were sometimes hundreds of miles away from their estates and hired stewards to run their properties. The atmosphere between master and serf on these lands depended, therefore, more on the relationship of the steward and the serf than on the nature of the absentee landowner. Another category of owner was made up of those—especially in the last years of legal serfdom—who bought and sold properties as speculative deals. Their only interest was money, and they did not concern themselves, except as it affected their profits, with the serfs.

Among the landowners, there were those who had humanitarian feelings, and they tried to treat their serfs with some show of kindness and understanding. Other landowners treated their serfs with a certain amount of decency simply because they were their property and they did not want to damage or destroy what belonged to them. Most important, since serf labor was the source of the master's ability to make money out of his lands, he had to make sure that they had the health and the strength to perform their work. Certainly, the serf could not depend upon government laws and regulations to guarantee that his master treated him decently.

Whatever few rights the law, in theory, allowed the serf were taken away from him in practice. For example, under a law passed in 1848, the serf, with the consent of his master, could accumulate real property. In practice, however, the lord could question the serf's ability to make payments and then confiscate his savings.

For example, a rich serf owned by Count Sheremetev died and left 150,000 rubles in bank deposits. The serf's children had bought their freedom from the count, but when they tried to have their father's money awarded to them, the count objected. The court ruled that since the dead serf had been owned by the count, all his possessions belonged to him, too, and awarded the money to the count.

The lord was forbidden to bring his serf to ruin. However, since the serf was forbidden to bring a civil suit against his master, in practice he had no way to defend himself against his lord.

The master's hold over the peasant extended to the very personal level as well as the economic and political. A master could refuse to grant permission for a marriage to be held on his estate or he could insist that a marriage take place between a boy and a girl that he had selected, whether they wished it or not. A master could insist on his right to spend the wedding night with the bride while the bridegroom spent the night with his friends. In some cases, the "right of the first night" was claimed by a steward when the lord was absent or when he did not wish to avail himself of the right.

When some foreign visitors to Russia in the nineteenth century referred to the serfs as "slaves," they were not reflecting an actual legal situation but, in some cases and in some ways, an actual condition. Many serfs did live under conditions usually associated with slavery. In fact, the Code of 1649, which was concerned with the welfare of slaves, was the basis for the next two hundred years for legislation regarding the obligations the proprietor owed his serfs. In the seventeenth-century code, the slaveowner had to feed his slaves during times of famine. If he failed to do so and the slave had to resort to begging, the slave could be taken away from his master. A master was forbidden to maim, torture, or starve to death a recaptured runaway slave.

For hundreds of years, the peasants had obligations to the landowners. These took the form of annual payments of money or products, known as *obrok*, and labor services, known as *barshchina*. In the early days, most of the obligations were obrok, mainly various kinds of crops such as rye and oats. In later years, the labor services increased in proportion to the annual payments. These obligations varied widely in different parts of Russia and in different times, but in general they involved a certain number of days each month in which the serf had to donate his labor to the master.

Over the years, the master-peasant relationship varied in detail but not in substance. In general, the landlord could allow the peasants a good deal of freedom in managing their affairs in the commune or he could reduce the amount of land allotted to the village as a whole or to any single householder. He could increase the amount of obrok or barshchina that he exacted from them. He could forbid his peasants to have economic relations with others outside the boundaries of his estate. He could pluck them from the land and make them domestic serfs. And finally, he could arrange or prevent marriages and sell them to another master. With all these severe restrictions, it is little wonder that the noble and serf were sometimes referred to as master and slave by foreigners visiting old Russia.

5 The Peasant

THE peasant *is* Russia. This observation about old Russia was a popular one not only because the peasants comprised 90 percent of the population, but because he, more than any other group, gave Russia its ethos. In sheer numbers alone, he dominated the villages and small towns. Even in the cities, the numbers of peasants continued to increase in relation to other groups.

The peasant's political power was virtually nonexistent. The overwhelming majority was illiterate. Economically, the peasant was the poorest of all; culturally, he was cut off from the more sophisticated Russian music, art, theater, and literature; socially, he was isolated from other classes in Russia. Yet, despite all this, it was the peasant who gave Russia its color, its character, and, in many ways, its outlook. In the expression, "Scratch a Russian and you will find a Tatar," one substitute could be "peasant" for Tatar. If one would scratch beneath the exterior of many Russian rulers, there was the suspicious, cruel, shrewd, obstinate Russian peasant. The czars Ivan the Terrible and Peter the Great seem to be closer to the peasant than to the conventionally urbane monarch.

Although the Russian peasant had his own unique qualities, he had a general affinity with other peasants of Europe. He was passionately attached to his land. He had a strong bond to his village and local community. His family relationships were strong. Marriage was tied closely to the economic condition of his life. The peasant father was a dominant figure. He had a deep distrust of "city folk." He was proudly religious and was tied to the church yet never lost his attraction for primitive ritual and superstitions. The list could be expanded almost endlessly.

In many ways, the peasant viewed life as "us and them." The peasant's own world was neat and ordered and comprehensible. The world of the non-peasant was chaotic, confused, and difficult to understand. To the Russian peasant, the rest of Europe was composed of *Nyemtsi* (Germans) and the rest of the world consisted of *Pravoslavniye* (Greek Orthodox), *Busurmanye* (Muhammadans), and *Poliacki* (Poles).

Although in the broad sense there was a class of people referred to as the "Russian peasant," actually the peasants varied in many ways. For example, as has already been mentioned, some peasants worked in the households of their masters, others were field serfs, still others were crown peasants, and some, especially in Siberia, were quite independent. There were peasants who lived in the country and those who lived in the city. Some were artisans, some worked in factories, and a few were actors, musicians, and artists.

There were kulaks, rich peasants with large land holdings who were often loansharks and consequently influenced greatly the economic life of the village. And there were the *batraki,* the poor rural proletariat, who were landless and worked for the landlords and kulaks.

In fact, there were so many types of peasants and such a variety of customs from one section to another in the vast domain of Russia that there is a saying that "each village has ways of its own."

The peasant in Siberia near the Yenisei River varied from the peasant of the Ukraine, the peasant on the large estates near Moscow, or the peasants of the Don. In the north, the peasant might be thin and sharp-featured and speak in the dialect of the Great Russian. In the southern districts, he might be dark, broad-faced, and broad-shouldered and speak the Little Russian dialect.

There was a strong unity, however, in the midst of all this diversity of work, geographic location, appearance, speech, and material possessions. And this unity revolved about the fact that the overwhelming majority, in spite of certain differences, formed a distinct economic and cultural group in Russian society. No other group in Russia had as long and continuous history. The middle class, the merchants, and intellectuals were relatively new groups in old Russia. Even the nobility, the other long-lived group, had changed drastically over the centuries from warrior-princes to Europeanized esthetes, nationalistic philosophers, or bureaucratic officeholders. The centuries-long affinity to the land—even among those peasants who worked in the cities—was a powerful unifying factor. Peasant agriculture was not only a means of earning a living; it was a way of life.

For all its poverty, suffering, oppression, and ignorance, this peasant way of life was not all pain. In his own way, the peasant had his moments of fullness and vitality. He had his rituals, his Orthodox religious pageantry, and his primitive superstitions and folklore. He had a close family life and a flourishing communal existence in the mir. There were the joys of the flesh, the camaraderie of the bathhouse and tavern, and the simple pleasures of fishing, weddings, birthdays, and holidays.

Above all, he did not live the lonely life of, for instance, an American pioneer family or a solitary farmer in an out-of-the-way area. The smallest Russian settlement had the characteristics of a close family and community. A single peasant household usually had a large number of persons and was almost a village in itself.

The patriarchal household usually included not only the children and grandchildren of the head of the family but other relatives by blood and marriage. Frequently, there were nonrelatives who had become part of the household and had become integrated into its economic and social setup.

Although many peasants were sold by their masters, the majority of peasants lived on the master's estates from one generation to the next. This gave them a feeling of "belonging," of being at one with the land, the community, and the special, intimate life of the particular area. This generations-long sense of belonging tended to make the peasant regard time as cyclical, an endless round of life, death, and rebirth. All this had its effect by making him more resigned about life and at peace with his surroundings and condition.

Still, despite the various positive or pleasant aspects of peasant life, the economic and political conditions of old Russia were so miserable that the bad far outweighed the good. Combined with the economic privation, political oppression, and social ostracism was the very nature of primitive rural life itself. This life was not idyllic or peaceful. The difficulties were overwhelming. Almost from birth, the peasant was faced with a hostile environment that could mean droughts and starvation or floods and destruction. He was continually plagued by an authoritarian father, a bureaucratic official, or a powerful landlord. His life was held cheap. He was cannon fodder for the czar's army and a soul to be bargained over, paid for, and sent to distant areas. He was for all intents and purposes a faceless man without rights and without hope.

All these difficulties forced him to fall back on his wits if he wished to survive at all. It is no wonder that the peasant became known as a man who was patient, cautious, suspicious, shrewd, ruthless, dishonest, and even treacherous. In effect, he was what he had to be in order to survive the ravages of both nature and man. A few rebelled against their fate by running away to other areas, especially Siberia. The overwhelming majority, however, continued to lead their mostly painful lives that extended in pitiful monotony between the time of their birth to the time of their death.

The peasant character and life intrigued the writers of Russia, who tried to understand and explain them in their stories and plays.

Leo Tolstoy viewed the peasant in all his primitiveness as a man who had learned to accept life and death in a humane and truthful way. He felt that the peasant in his innocence had much native wisdom to impart to others in Russian society.

Feodor Dostoevsky looked into the peasant soul and suggested that light and salvation for Russia might well come from the lower classes, especially the peasant. "He will teach you how to live and die," Dostoevsky is reported to have said about the Russian peasant.

Anton Chekhov saw the peasant as neither a man of great wisdom nor of stupefying idiocy. He portrayed him as quite a prosaic individual, who lived his life as best he could under difficult circumstances.

Maxim Gorky saw him as a victim of a brutal, dehumanizing situation in which he became depraved and brutalized. Gorky felt the only way out for the peasant was to change the conditions that had desolated him as a man. In his pamphlet *On the Russian Peasantry,* he both pities and condemns the peasant for what centuries of Russian life had done to him.

> The boundless plain [Gorky wrote] upon which the log-walled, thatch-roofed village huts stand huddled together has the poisonous property of desolating a man's soul and draining him of all desire for action. The peasant may go beyond the limits of his village, take a look at the emptiness all about him, and after a while he will feel as if this desolation had entered into his own soul. Nowhere are lasting traces of toil to be seen. The estates of the landlords? But they are few, and enemies live there. The cities? But they are far away, and culturally not much more important than the village. As far as the eye can see stretches an endless plain, and in the midst of it stands an insignificant wretched little man, cast away upon this dreary earth to labor like a galley slave. And the man is overwhelmed by a feeling of indifference which kills his capacity to think, to remember past experience, and to draw inspiration from it.

Ivan Bunin viewed him as a "nothing man," one who had become dehumanized and inhumane because of poverty, oppression, and ignorance.

The peasant's own view of his life, however, was often quite matter-of-fact. He rarely concerned himself with matters that the intellectuals foisted on him—philosophy, soul, destiny. For the millions of peasants, life was a daily grind—a day-to-day struggle to provide himself and his family with the bare necessities of life.

6 Economy and Work

W HEREVER people live close to the soil and depend upon its fertility for their existence, there is a close, sometimes almost mystical, bond between man and the earth. The Russian peasant's love for his land was legendary. He spoke of it with affection and devotion as one would of one's lover or children. His speech and songs were full of endearments for the land. He referred to it as "little mother" or just "mother." His thoughts suggested that he wanted to serve the land properly and not to abuse it for his own advantage.

Although he did not wish to abuse the land, the primitiveness of his tools forced him to abuse himself in working the land he loved. Often he did not have a horse to pull his plow and he had to harness himself to it. Even if he was fortunate enough to have a horse, his working hours were long, and the yield, because of the backwardness of his agricultural methods, was often meager. He was almost totally unaware of new agricultural procedures that were coming more and more into use in advanced countries. It was said that "in the primitive system of agriculture usually practiced in Russia, the natural labor-unit . . . comprises a man, a woman, and a horse."

Actually, it would be more accurate to say one-half a man, a woman, and a horse, because in most peasant communities at least half of the male population was away, either in the army or working in the cities to help augment the family income.

In most parts of Russia, the three-field system was in use. This meant that the arable part of the land, say, in a commune, was divided into three large fields. Each field was then cut up into long narrow strips and one or more were allocated, according to the decision of the village assembly, to individual households. In a fairly typical situation, the first field was set aside for a winter grain—for instance, rye, which was the staple grain for bread. The second field might be planted with oats to feed the horses and buckwheat for their own food. The third would lie fallow and was used during the summer as a pasture for cattle. This triennial system allowed for the field that was used one year for raising winter grain to be used the next year for raising summer grain. The third year, it would lie fallow.

The agriculture year in northern Russia began in April, after the melting of the snow. In late April, the cattle were taken from the cowsheds and sprinkled with holy water by the village priest. As D. MacKenzie Wallace points out, the cattle, fed almost exclusively on straw during the long winter, "look like the ghosts of their former emaciated selves. All are lean and weak, many are lame, and some cannot rise to their feet without assistance."

The field for the summer grain was now plowed. This task took until the end of May. The fallow field for the winter grain was then spread with manure. At the end of June, haymaking began. This was followed by the harvest, which lasted until the end of August. During this period, the peasant worked day and night in order to finish reaping and stacking summer grain and sowing the winter grain for the following year. At the end of September, his labor in the fields was over and on the first of October the harvest festival began.

This was one of the most joyous times of the year. If the season was good, beer, cakes, pies, and other foods were served after the traditional long ceremonies at the church. After the feast, the young people sang and played, the older folk gossiped and vowed eternal friendship toward each other. The drinking of vodka was truly prodigious, and, as Wallace notes, they "stagger about aimlessly in besotted self-contentment, till they drop down in a state of complete unconsciousness. There they will lie tranquilly till they are picked up by their less intoxicated friends, or more probably till they awake of their own accord on the next morning."

From the time of the autumn harvest festival until the following spring, the peasant family had no agricultural work to do. Some peasants would spend their time idly, lounging for hours at a time on the shelf above the stove. Some would try to get work transporting grain. Others would go to the city to find employment. Still other peasants and their family would engage themselves in one or another kind of handicraft.

Peasants pose with their ox, used for plowing.

Sovfoto

Sowing in the traditional manner.

Tass from Sovfoto

Peasant handicrafts were found throughout Russia, and many peasants spent part or all of their time in this work in both the villages and the cities. In fact, the number of peasants who never tilled a field but devoted all of their time to handicrafts numbered in the millions. They made an almost endless variety of goods in bark, wood, cloth, leather, felt, clay, and metal. Some of the products were crude and imitative; others were excellent examples of peasant science and peasant art. The products varied from simple objects such as wooden snow shovels, brooms made of twigs, felt boots, and unglazed milk pots to artistically rendered silver ornaments and religious pictures. There was scarcely a village or city bazaar in all of Russia that was not filled with a wide variety of handicrafts fashioned by the peasants.

In some cases, the production of handicrafts was carried on in the huts of the peasants. Sometimes, a small cooperative shop was set up by a group of peasant workers. In other cases, a master would hire the peasants and pay them wages. Quite often, an entrepreneur would make a deal with a peasant family for its output of handicrafts. At other times, the peasant himself took his goods to the market. During the long winter months, it was not unusual for an entire peasant family to be hard at work on handicrafts in order to supplement its meager income from agriculture.

Although peasant handicrafts existed in Russia for a long time, it was only at the beginning of the seventeenth century that they became an important supplement to the peasant's income. By the middle of the eighteenth century, handicraft production had become a flourishing industry, especially in the villages. After 1850, with the spread of the factory system and the increased production of factory-made goods, handicraft production eased off somewhat. Even so, peasant labor was so cheap that in many cases the hand-made commodity could compete successfully with those made by machines. Although there are few reliable statistics in this area for the time, it is probably true that in the nineteenth century the total value of the peasant handicraft production was greater than the value of the output of Russia's factories.

In addition to agriculture and handicrafts, a large number of peasants were engaged in manufacturing and mining. As the number of factories and mines increased, a greater number of peasants were needed to work in them. As pathetically inadequate as the wages in these industries were, they still offered, in many cases, a better income than the peasant could expect from his work in agriculture. The life of the peasant as a worker in the city will be described later. We have already seen, however, that as far as his work was concerned, the peasant was certainly not only a farmer. In fact, in some cases he was not a worker either, but an entrepreneur—a merchant.

The peasant-as-merchant has been a part of the Russian scene for as long a time as the peasant class itself. There were always some shrewd peasants who realized that it was easier and more profitable to trade goods made by others than to make the goods themselves. However, in early days, the laws against peasants becoming merchants were severe. Even so, some peasants, by initiative and wit, managed to become merchants. By the middle of the eighteenth century, the government recognized its inability to restrict the peasant merchant, and the laws became more permissive in this regard. By the early nineteenth century, the peasant, in ef-

Spinning silk in the years before the revolution.

fect, had as much right to engage in trade as did a member of the merchant class.

The growing right of the peasant to engage in commerce was not the result of the government's wish to please him but rather the result of its recognition that the growth of Russian commerce itself depended to an extent on the intrepid peasant merchant. Used to the hard life, the peasant-as-merchant was to be found in the most wild and primitive settlements in Siberia as well as in the villages and cities of European Russia. In the cities, there were shops owned by peasants. In fact, as early as the middle of the eighteenth century, delegates to the Legislative Commission —called by Catherine the Great in 1767 to formulate a new law code for the empire—complained that "peasants had moved into cities with their families and had opened shops selling all manner of goods, including luxury wares and imported products, and were active, too, in wholesale trade."

In those cases where the laws prevented the peasant merchant from operating or owning shops in the cities, he often conspired with his master so that he could circumvent the law for his own and his master's profit. For example, in Moscow and St. Petersburg, where each building had a plaque with the name of the owner on it, all the buildings in one of the streets of the merchants' quarter were reputed to have had on them the name of Sheremetev or Orlov, two great families among the Russian gentry. In fact, however, they were the homes and shops of their serfs, who had made arrangements to purchase the buildings in their masters' names since it was illegal for serfs to own real property in their own names.

Nevertheless, despite the number of peasants engaged in handicrafts, mining, manufacturing, or commerce, old Russia was still a country in which the peasant-as-farmer living in dilapidated huts in dreary villages was the predominant peasant way of life. Accounts of the poverty-stricken peasants in poverty-stricken villages vary little, whether written in the seventeenth century or the early twentieth century. Over these three hundred years or so, the material conditions of the peasants changed little. Similarly, the way the peasant worked his land and the tools he used to cultivate it changed little from century to century.

The *sokha,* for example—a wooden hook plow of ancient design —was used in the sixteenth century and was still widely used in the early twentieth century. Because of its light weight and inefficient design, it could cut only a shallow furrow and could not turn over large clods or efficiently tear up weed roots. The sickle was widely used for harvesting cereals, and the scythe was used for cutting hay and, sometimes, grain. Threshing was done with flails.

One of the accounts of the peasant's agricultural tools, written by the Frenchman Chantreau after his visit to Russia in 1788, tells of the tools he saw outside a peasant's hut:

> We amused ourselves with examining a plough and harrow at his door. We could not enough admire the workmanship. The plough was the simplest thing imaginable and the harrow was nothing but a collection of trunks of young fir trees. If these instruments be attended with the least possible expense, it must be acknowledged at the same time, that they are weak and insufficient for tearing from the earth the fruits demanded of it; for they reach only to the surface, and in this climate the earth must be tormented, not caressed.

Equally primitive vehicles were used to transport crops from the field or, for that matter, firewood from the forests or a fishing catch from the lakes or streams. These were usually crude two- or four-wheel carts, sledges, sleighs, and boats of simple construction. It was only in the nineteenth century that the more wealthy peasants began to use carriages that might have springs and a collapsible top and were pulled by from one to three horses.

The kinds of crops, like the tools themselves, had changed little over the centuries. The principal crops were cereals—rye, wheat, barley, oats, millet, and buckwheat. In addition to cereals, flax and hemp were the most important crops. Except for the commercial sale of vegetables in nearby cities, vegetables were raised in small gardens for the consumption of the members of the peasant household. Certain vegetables, such as potatoes and cucumbers, were favorites. One Englishman in the early nineteenth century noted that in the summer nearly every peasant he saw had

Peasant woman cutting wheat in Central Russia.

UPI

"a bit of black bread in one hand and a cucumber in the other."

The farm animals were among the poorest and scrawniest to be seen anywhere. The peasants usually overworked their horses, when they had any, and fed and maintained them poorly. Their horses have been described as "small, weak-limbed, and weak-boned creatures inadequate for the heavy work." The cattle, usually light in weight and of poor quality, were used as work animals as well as for milking. Like most of the more backward countries of Europe at the time, there was little interest in animal husbandry on the part of either landowner or peasant. No attention was paid to selective breeding; the animals were fed poorly and treated with little care. In moderate weather, they were turned out-of-doors to fend for themselves in the common pasture. In the winter, they were kept in miserably cold sheds and fed mainly straw.

The combination of adverse weather conditions, such as drought and floods, the unconcern of master and peasant alike toward upgrading methods of tillage, primitive tools, inadequate fertilization, and the poor quality of farm animals resulted in low crop yields at best and famine conditions at worst. In addition, the transportation system of the empire was incredibly poor. Farm products often spoiled before they reached the market or, in some cases, they never got there at all because of the trouble and expense of driving primitive carts over impossible roads.

Irrigation was minimal or nonexistent. As a result, inadequate rainfall often resulted in partial or almost total crop failures. In the eighteenth century, it is estimated there were thirty-four partial or general crop failures. In the early part of the nineteenth century, comparative data revealed that the Russian crop yields were lower than those of any other European nation.

As a result of all these factors, the income of the peasant even as late as the middle of the nineteenth century was estimated to be, depending on the area of the country, from 40 to 70 percent of his minimal requirements. To keep from starvation, it was imperative that he supplement his farm income with additional income from handicrafts, work in the city, or seasonal wage-work in agriculture outside of his village.

From his inadequate income, the peasant, it must be remembered, was forced to meet his obligations to his master and his taxes to the state. On those estates where the main obligations were in the form of forced labor, or barshchina, adults of both sexes usually were required to work for the master a minimum of three days a week. In some cases, they had to work as many as four or five, while the peasant's own crop rotted in the ground. In addition, it was customary for the peasant to have to give his master payment in kind, too—poultry, eggs, meat, honey, homespun cloth, and the like.

Where the landlords required that the peasants fulfill their obligations by giving him an annual payment of money, the amount varied, depending on the era and whether or not the peasant was also obligated to do forced labor.

Every male peasant, whether he was a serf or a state peasant, had to pay a soul tax or have it paid for him. This tax was levied on all non-nobles, even on those persons who had died since the last collection, the so-called dead souls of Gogol's famous novel of the same name. On privately owned estates, the serf owner had the task of collecting the tax for the government. Among state peasants, the commune had the responsibility to collect and transmit the soul tax of the male members of the mir.

In addition to his obligations of obrok, barshchina, or both, to his master, and a soul tax to the state, the peasant had to pay a host of indirect taxes. Over the years, these indirect or excise taxes steadily increased until by the beginning of the twentieth century they made up a large part of the revenue of the state treasury. Products taxed included vodka, sugar, tobacco, kerosene, and even matches. Generally, these were items of widespread, popular consumption. To illustrate the everyday necessities that were taxed, the American historian G. T. Robinson noted:

> When the peasant could afford a luxurious evening, he filled his lamp with taxed kerosene (if he had a lamp), lighted it with a taxed match (or with a splinter from the stove), poured a little taxed tobacco into a cigarette paper, also taxed (or into a cone of newspaper), and puffed himself into a cloud of smoke. If this operation made him thirsty, he drank a glass of taxed tea, with a lump of taxed sugar gripped between his teeth. Or perhaps he went out to buy a bottle of

vodka . . . drank off the liquor in large gulps from the bottle-mouth or from a tea-glass; and as a result of this act of consumption, the state received a handsome revenue in its double capacity of tax-collector and of merchant under the Spirit Monopoly.

It is no wonder, therefore, that the peasant was almost always in debt. Stepniak wrote that the peasant of mid-nineteenth-century Russia was in constant indebtedness, either to his master, the steward, the kulak, or a professional moneylender. The peasant was convinced that once he allowed himself to get into debt, he would remain in bondage to the end of his days.

By and large, this was true. The interest rates charged for loans were unbelievably high. In Ivan the Terrible's day, they were often as high as 156 percent, and sometimes they were as high as 1 percent a day. In later years, they were not so outrageous, but they were still exorbitant. The peasant was often forced to enter into what was known as a *kabala* [servitude or bondage] contract in which not only he but his entire family were liable. In some cases, all members of the family had to give their labor to work off the debt, which often remained charged against the family for the rest of their lives. In effect, it often took two generations—the parents and their children—to pay off the debt. In some cases, both a father and son borrowed money, and thus the two-generation payment was also maintained. Quite often, the contract stated that the peasant had to work continuously for his creditor until the debt was paid. The creditor, for his part, was obliged to feed and clothe him. In actuality, therefore, the debtor became a life-long peon of his creditor, since his labor usually paid only the interest on the debt, not the principal itself. In a sense, he became a slave and, in fact, was often referred to as a kabala slave.

The state required a certain number of peasants to report for military service. During the time of Peter the Great, peasants were conscripted without the permission of their owners. Later, the number of recruits was a percentage from each settlement or village. Usually, the recruits were chosen by lot. Over the years, this varied from one recruit for every one hundred males to seven for every one thousand males, except in wartime when the quotas were considerably increased.

A young peasant conscript leaves to join the army.

The age of the recruits was originally from twenty to thirty-five years old, but in the 1850s it was reduced to men under thirty-one and not less than sixty-three inches tall. During the eighteenth century, peasants were recruited for life. In subsequent years, the term of service was reduced to twenty-five years, then to twenty plus five years of ready reserve in the militia, and by 1855 to twelve years of active service and three years in the militia.

The village was required to outfit the recruits and pay their transportation to the military post. If a peasant was chosen for military service and he could afford to buy a substitute, this was allowed, since recruitment was not by the individual but by the number of men from each village. In addition to buying substitutes, all kinds of other ruses were used to avoid military service. Sometimes in order to keep a peasant from the service, a master would send him to another of his properties or he would have him transferred to a relative or friend. Often, to keep his best peasants, the master would make sure that idlers and troublemakers were taken instead by the recruiting officers.

Peasants often mutilated themselves to keep out of the army or crippled their children to make them unfit for service. If it was discovered that a peasant had mutilated himself to avoid service, he was forced to run three times through a gauntlet of five hundred soldiers armed with whips. If he was still able-bodied, he was then sent into the army and given the most dangerous assignments. If he could not walk satisfactorily, he was made a driver. If he had mutilated himself to the point where he was totally unfit for military service, he was whipped and sentenced to hard labor for the rest of his life. Ironically, the settlement or village was given credit for completely mutilated recruits as well as for those who were able-bodied.

7 The Family

THE peasant family has been compared to a labor association with all members having all things in common. All members worked toward a common economic goal, and no one, not even the khozain, the head of the family, could dispose of the family's crops or goods without the consent of the other adult males of the household. Illegitimate sons in the household, if they were working, contributing members, had the same rights as the legitimate sons, even to sharing in the inheritance. This inheritance, upon the death of the khozain, was distributed equally to all male members of the family.

Although all male members of the family had a say in the economic affairs of the household, the male head of the family, whether the father or grandfather, had an almost autocratic power over the other members. He was as much the autocratic patriarch as the old Hebraic father figure or the reigning head of a noble family. This authority had no basis in law but was a natural authority that had been established by custom and usage. Outside his house, the father was tightly bound by all the laws, regulations, and customs that existed in the region and the empire. However, inside his own family, he answered, it was said, only to God.

His tasks and responsibilities within his family were many and varied. He distributed the work tasks and judged whether they were properly done. He guarded the family's traditions and morals. He represented the household at the village assembly. As the head of a miniature totalitarian state, he was the final arbiter in family affairs and disputes. His word was law, and there was no recourse but to accept his decisions. The village would not interfere, except on the father's side, if he needed help with, say, a recalcitrant son. Courts rarely acted on complaints of children against parents. Their view was that the father was necessarily right and that his authority was sacred. Rebellion against, or even resistance to, his will was both a crime and a sin.

There is the case, for example, of a peasant in the Ukraine in the early part of the twentieth century who drowned his disobedient son. The peasant was tried by the rural court, was found guilty, and sentenced to three months in jail. The verdict was based not on the fact that he murdered his son but for "failing to bring the boy up in the sacred virtue of filial obedience."

Although the male head of the household was a supreme autocrat, this condition was not unique to the Russian peasant. In colonial America, a contemporary observer wrote, "without exception, the husband is master over the house; as touching his family he had more authority than a king in his kingdome." The Puritan child was taught that it was his duty, by Scripture, to obey. His will to resist, wrote one commentator, "was broken by persistent and adequate punishment. He was taught it was a sin to find fault with his meals, his apparel, his tasks, or his lot in life." And in the Old Testament it is noted that "if a man has a stubborn and rebellious son, which will not obey the voice of his father, or the voice of his mother, and that, when they have chastened him, will not hearken unto them: Then shall his father and mother lay hold on him, and bring him out unto the elders of his city . . . and all the men of his city shall stone him with stones, that he die. . . ."

This autocratic view still persists in many primitive parts of the world, even in certain isolated mountain areas of present-day United States.

The head of the Russian peasant family had a tyrannical hold on the other members of his family. The wife, for instance, was often beaten if she did not act as her husband believed was proper. His dominance began on their wedding day, when the husband was given a knout by the bride's father as a symbol—and sometimes as an actual weapon—of his dominance over her.

Yet in many cases a wife did share authority—and dignity—with her husband. Although he was the master in economic affairs, the wife was usually the master of the household itself and was in charge of raising the children. In many respects, she was the mainstay of the peasant family. She not only did the household chores but often engaged in handicraft work as well. And during the agricultural season, the wife and other women of the household worked side by side with their men in the fields.

Wives often ran the entire household and exercised authority—including the economic part—during the frequent and lengthy absences of their husbands in the city or in the army. In effect, she was often the dominant figure in the household. In later-day Russian culture and literature, the *matushka,* mother, was a symbol of endurance, love, and the supreme binding force in the family.

Among the women members of the peasant family, the daughter-in-law had the least enviable position. Upon marriage, she was taken by her new husband to the home of his parents. There, she had a position of little more than a household slave to the mother, who transferred to her the hardships and difficulties she herself might have suffered at the hands of her husband. In the traditional peasant marriage, love had little to do with marriage. The bride was supposed to bring to the marriage, and to the household, two strong arms and a willingness to work. Sometimes, in order to get this pair of strong arms, a young boy was married to her. It was not unheard of, wrote one commentator, for a strapping bride to carry her little husband in her arms. Under such circumstances, it was not uncommon for the head of the family to take as his mistress the wife of his young son.

The abuse of the daughter-in-law has been written about in many Russian stories and was a frequent subject of folk stories and sayings. Among the Little Russians, for instance, there was a characteristic anecdote: "Who is going to bring the water? The daughter-in-law. Who is going to be beaten? The daughter-in-law. Why is she beaten? Because she is the daughter-in-law."

The position of women, in general, in old Russia was not enviable. Except in those cases where a strong-willed, forceful woman pushed herself into a position of dignity or some authority, their lot was pathetic. At best, they were considered the inferior of men and at worst an object of derision. In old Russia, there are hundreds of disparaging sayings about women. A few of them are:

> Beat your fur overcoat and it will be warmer; beat your wife and she will be sweeter.
> I love thee like my soul, and I dust thee like my jacket.
> Beat your wife with the butt end of the axe, then sniff; if she breathes, she is fooling you and wants more.
> A wife is loved on two occasions: once, when you marry her, and again, when you take her to the grave.
> There is no law for women or for cattle.
> The more you beat your woman, the better the soup will taste.
> A chicken is not a bird, and a woman is not a human being.
> In ten women there is but one soul.

Actually, according to the official tax collectors, women did not have even a tenth part of a soul. Only men had souls and therefore had to pay taxes. The "soul tax" did not apply to women.

Toward the end of the nineteenth century, peasant women began to rebel against the tyranny of their husbands. In some cases, they even traded blow for blow when they were beaten. A popular ditty of the time reflected this new feeling among women. The woman says: "You squint horribly. / I'm not afraid of you. / You dare not knock me down." When the fight does break out, however, the ditty continues: "The husband let out with his hand, / And boxed his wife upon the ear. / The wife she let out with her hand, / And hit him right across the face."

Russia, unlike many parts of Europe, did not have an Age of Chivalry. Until the nineteenth century, there was little or no tradition or literature in which the gentleman paid homage to his lady. There was no poetry that spoke of gentle ladies and undying love. Characteristics of gentility, daintiness, compassion—so often considered to be feminine traits—were not part of many women in old Russia. For instance, an eighteenth-century traveler noted "that in Russia the women are usually more spiteful, more cruel, and more barbarous than the men: and it is because they are still much more ignorant and more superstitious."

The young children of the family were expected at an early age to share in the work and to do their tasks well. They were trained to respect the authority of their elders, especially the father. They were made to realize that their work, as little as it might be, was important to the marginal existence that was the lot of most peasant families.

Until he was about the age of seven, the boy lived a more or less carefree life. After that, he was required to help in whatever work

Russian peasant women pulling a raft.

Sovfoto

was assigned to him. Training in obedience came early. The peasant believed, as the Russian saying put it, that "if you don't teach the child when he lies across the width of the sleeping bench, then you will not be able to teach him when he stretches out on the whole length of the bench."

The girls of the family had life a little easier and enjoyed more freedom than the boys. Since marriage was the goal of every girl and that meant that she would be leaving the household eventually for the house of her husband, she was regarded as a temporary worker in the household. If the father died before the daughters were married, it was the duty of her older brothers to outfit her suitably for her marriage.

Marriage came early—often at the age of fifteen for a girl and eighteen for a boy.

Many analogies exist between the peasant family of old Russia as an entity and the communes in which many of them lived. In both social units, there were common interests and common responsibilities. In both organizations, there was a principal person who headed the group; in the family it was the khozain and in the mir it was the starosta. Both had limited authority. In the case of the khozain, his authority was limited by the other male members of the family; in the case of the starosta, it was limited by the other heads of the households. In both instances, too, there was common property. In the family, it consisted of the hut and most of its contents; in the mir, it was the arable land and pasturage. Both groups also had a common responsibility for taxes and debts.

There were fundamental differences, too. The family was a close-knit group and the mir was a loose-knit group. Probably most fundamental was the fact that the family worked as a unified group, all farming together and sharing their earnings from a common purse. In the mir, each household farmed independently of the other and paid into the commune's treasury a limited sum.

These similarities and differences were to play an important role in determining the reactions of the peasants to the collectivization of agriculture instituted by the Communists some years after the Revolution of 1917.

8 The Peasant Condition

FROM century to century, the political, social, and economic conditions of the Russian peasant worsened. There were, for instance, more free peasants in the days of Ivan the Terrible than in the days of Catherine the Great. Wave after wave of repressive laws strangled the peasant's freedom of movement. Socially, his inferior position in Russian society was symbolized by an ill-clad peasant with his hat in his hand and his head bowed in obeisance to his master and his czar. Though a small number had managed to escape poverty, the overwhelming mass of Russian peasants was deep in the mire of privation. Excerpts from a mid-nineteenth-century government study commission on the condition of the Russian peasant in the province of Viatka noted:

> Pankret Horev and wife have a family of six daughters and one son, all under age. He is the only full-grown workman in the house. He pays taxes for two souls. His property: one cow, one horse, two sheep. ... Means of subsistence: knows no trade. Have ground their last sack of oats.

Hungry peasants during the time of the czar.

Ivan Jkanov: Family of five people, with one full-grown workman. His property: one cow, one horse, one sheep. Means of subsistence: no bread since the autumn. Begs with his children. In order to pay off second installment of his taxes has sold his hay.

Emelian Jkanov: A family of ten people, of which one is a full-grown workman. Pays for one and a half souls. His property: no cow, no horse, the house in ruins—uninhabitable. Means of subsistence: begging. To pay the taxes has sold his last horse.

Many peasants ran away to escape from their poverty. In some cases, they were caught and returned to their master. In other cases, if their escape was successful, their lives were as poverty-stricken in their new locations as in the ones they left. Often, they arrived at their new home with nothing but the rags on their back, or as writers described them, "as arriving with nothing and bringing with them only body and soul."

Those peasants who did not run away had no incentive to work hard on their lands. The mounting burden of taxes to the state and dues to their lord left them almost nothing for their families. They were defeated and without hope. Giles Fletcher, an Englishman who spent many years in Russia in the late sixteenth century and who wrote one of the best descriptions of the Russia of that period, observed even then the utter despair and helplessness of the Russian peasant:

"Concerning the landes, goods, and other possessions of the commons," he wrote, "they assume the name and lie common indeed without any fence against the rapine and spoile, not only of the highest [the czar] but of his nobilities, officers and souldiers. . . . This maketh the people (though otherwise hardened to beare any toile) to give themselves much to idleness and drinking."

Poverty often resulted in hunger, and hunger sometimes became starvation. Stepniak noted that it was not unusual for the "ordinary run of villagers, during eight months out of the twelve, to eat bread mixed with husks, pounded straw, or birch bark." He quotes a peasant as saying, "The children are not like cattle. You cannot cut their throats and eat them when there is no forage for them. Willing or unwilling, you must feed them."

During the famine of 1892, the Russian nobleman Von Birukoff reported a peasant as saying:

> We got something, little father, but it is not enough. It was too little from the first. Then we borrowed. When we got more from the committee we had first to pay back what we had borrowed, so that there remained still less than before. The first week of the month we have enough to still our hunger, but the other weeks we have to starve. What have we not eaten! We dug clay, which we mixed with a little flour, but all kinds of clay are not suitable.

Conditions of starvation and hunger forced many Russian peasants to beg. These "beggars" were not full-time professional beggars, of which there were many in Russia. These were working peasants whose labor had resulted not in well-being but in hunger.

One late-nineteenth-century writer had described this begging for "morsels" as follows:

> By the end of December about thirty couples came every day and

begged for morsels. Among them were children and old people, also strong lads and maidens. Hunger is a hard master; a fasting man will sell the saints, say the muzhiks. A young man or girl feels reluctant and ashamed to beg, but there is no help for it. There is nothing, literally nothing, to eat at home. Today they have eaten the last loaf of bread, from which they yesterday cut "morsels" for those who knocked at their door. No bread, no work. . . .

A man who seeks "for morsels" and a regular beggar belong to two entirely different types of people. A beggar is a professional man; begging is his trade. A beggar has no land, no house, no permanent abiding place, for he is constantly wandering from one place to another. . . . He is generally a cripple, a sickly man incapable of work, a feeble old man, or a fool: he is clad in rags, and begs in a loud voice, sometimes in an importunate way, and is not ashamed of his calling. A beggar is God's man. . . .

A man, however, who asks "for morsels" is of quite another class. He is a peasant from the neighborhood. He is clothed like all his brother peasants, sometimes, in a new *armiak:* a linen sack slung over his shoulder is his only distinguishing mark. . . .

He enters the house as if by accident, and on no particular business beyond warming himself a little; and the mistress of the house, so as not to offend his modesty, will give him "the morsel" incidentally, and "unawares." If the man comes at dinner time he is invited to table. The muzhik is very delicate in the management of such matters, because he knows that someday he, too, may perhaps have to seek out "morsels" on his own account. . . .

The man who calls for "a morsel" is ashamed to beg. On entering the izba he makes the sign of the cross and stops on the threshold in silence, or mutters in a low voice, "Give in Christ's name." Nobody pays any attention to him; all go on with their business, and chat or laugh as if nobody were there. Only the mistress approaches the table, picks up a piece of bread three square inches in size, and gives it to her visitor. He makes the sign of the cross and goes. All the pieces given are the same size—three square inches. If two people come together (they generally work in couples), the mistress puts the question, "Are you collecting together?" If the answer is "Yes," she gives them a piece of six square inches; if separately, she cuts the piece in two.

The man who tramps the neighborhood thus owns a house, and enjoys his allotted share of land; he is the owner of horses, cows, sheep, clothes, only for the moment he has no bread. When in ten months' time he carries his crops, he will not merely cease begging, but will himself be the giver of bread to others. If by means of the aid now afforded him he weathers the storm and succeeds in finding work, he will with the money he earns at once buy bread, and himself help those who have none. . . .

In addition to the hardships of hunger and the indignity of being forced to beg for a crust of bread, the peasant was subjected to many kinds of oppression and cruelty—some of them allowed by law and others by custom. It has already been pointed out that he had to pay the master various dues in money, kind, or labor. During the years of legal serfdom, he could be sold to another master or he could be taken from his family and made into a domestic servant in the master's employ or the employ of others. He could be taken into military service for years ranging, according to the era, from twelve years of active duty to lifetime duty. If he was incorrigible or a "troublemaker," he could be sent to Siberia at the insistence of his master. The law allowed the master to beat his serf without any interference by the authorities.

Even as late as 1898, more than a quarter of a century after serfdom was legally abolished, a list of grievances gathered from the peasants and given to Czar Nicholas II by Count Witte included the following abuses: arbitrary punishment that was usually corporal, arbitrary restrictions on leaving his village, the lack of clear definition of his legal rights, and oppression by government officials.

For hundreds of years, the peasants had complained that they were not treated justly. They insisted that laws referring to them were either partial to their masters or ignored in practice. Injustice was as great during the periods when the peasants had their own separate lower courts, where minor criminal and civil cases were tried in accordance with custom law. In practice, as one observer noted, "the law in these courts very often proved to be no law at all."

In the Russian system of justice, an accused peasant had little opportunity of defending himself. The courts of the empire, however, were meticulous in trying not to condemn a man in a formal trial unless all formal precautions were taken. As a result, there were endless delays and interminable investigations. During this period, which often extended for years between the time of the arrest and the time of the verdict, the accused languished in jail.

With such political, economic, and social injustices, it is no wonder that the peasant condition in two other areas—health and education—was deplorable.

Figures are not available specifically on the health of the peasantry. However, since the peasantry was about 90 percent of the population, the following fact is significant. In the first years of the twentieth century, the annual death rate for European Russia was 31.2 per thousand as compared with, for example, 19.6 in France and 16 in England.

In the rural areas, doctors were scarce and in the more isolated areas nonexistent. Herb medicine and homemade remedies were widely used. The village midwife delivered the babies, and the *feldsher,* a medical assistant, or the *znakharka* took care of the sick. A feldsher has been described as an "old soldier who dresses wounds and gives physic." A znakharka has been described as a "woman who is half witch, half medical practitioner—the whole permeated with a strong leaven of knavery."

In 1897, 80 percent of all Russian peasants—whether they lived in the country or the city—were illiterate. By 1913, four years before the revolution, it was estimated that 55 percent of the male peasants were illiterate. However, although literacy increased, the number of truly educated peasants was only a tiny fraction. A survey made in 1909 revealed that out of 107 typical peasant households where at least one member was "literate," only six spent as much as fifty cents a year on books.

Until 1827, it was forbidden to send a serf to a secondary school or a university. After that time, the same rule applied, except to those who had been set free. The few peasants who did manage to get a secondary school education or the infinitesimal few who managed to go to the university usually went abroad through the aid of their enlightened masters. Sometimes, a landlord maintained a school on his estate, where some peasants received education that would help them become clerks or surveyors or perform certain technical jobs. The peasants who were selected for these schools were usually house serfs.

Although most peasants were uneducated, they did have a store of knowledge that was not learned from books. Through experiences in his day-to-day life and through his traditions and customs, the Russian peasant had learned many things. He was an excellent storyteller. His store of folk songs was wide. His mechanical skills—the thatching of a roof, the repairing of a wagon, etc.—were often first-class. Through the mir, he had learned how to act jointly with his neighbors on matters that affected their village and their economy. Perhaps most significantly, he developed a native cunning and shrewdness, which even the best schools could not teach their students.

9 Customs

VISITORS to old Russia have remarked on the fact that the Russian peasant was easily identifiable because of his very special customs and life style. Russian writers have devoted a great deal of attention to describing various aspects of peasant life that, in total, gave it a special identity, so different from that of other groups in Russian society.

One of the most noticeable aspects of the peasant, especially to foreigners, was his hospitality. This was—and is—a characteristic of almost all Russians. However, the hospitality of a poverty-stricken peasant who would insist on cooking his last chicken for his guests was especially heart-warming. Although poor, he entertained and welcomed members of his family, holy men and pilgrims, neighbors, and beggars with kindness, graciousness, warmth, and "in the name of God."

When food and drink were available, the peasant loved to indulge his appetites and was overjoyed to share his good fortune with others. "Bring to the table everything you can find in the oven," was a saying that was based on reality. He firmly believed, as he put it, that "a house is not made beautiful by its room but by its pies." Feasts would often last an entire day. During all this time, the peasant and his guest would eat, rest, then eat some more while the girls danced, the boys horsed around, folk songs were sung, and several musical instruments were played, including the balalaika and the concertina.

Although the peasant could be quarrelsome—during which time he was unexcelled in his colorful use of off-color language—most of the time he was extremely polite to his fellow peasants as well as to his masters. The Frenchman Chantreau during his visit to late-eighteenth-century Russia was impressed by the fact that "when peasants meet they lift their hats, bow frequently, and with much ceremony. In common conversation, they speak with much action, never give over making gestures, and in particular express respect for their superiors in the most servile way."

Except for holidays or special occasions such as weddings or birthdays, the day-to-day diet of the poor peasant varied little. The staple of his diet was rye bread, often referred to as "black bread," although it was actually not black but dark brown. It was pleasant to the taste and very nourishing. Persons unaccustomed to it found it hard to digest and often suffered severe stomach pains after eating a good deal of it. The peasants, however, could eat pounds of it at a time with no ill effects.

Chantreau observed that "their rye bread at first offends the eye but it is nourishing good. When people are accustomed to it, there is nothing disagreeable about it. If they be hungry, they think it excellent; if they have travelled forty versts, without getting anything, they think it delicious." A century later, Haxthausen noted that "the principal food of the Russian people consists of bread; potatoes are unknown in most districts. . . . Each soldier receives two and a half pounds of bread a day. A healthy Russian peasant cannot subsist without three pounds; and in the harvest he eats five pounds."

Next to bread, vegetables were the most important item in the peasant's diet. And the most widely eaten vegetable was cabbage, which was usually made into a kind of thick soup. Mushrooms and cucumbers, which were plentiful in many parts of Russia, were also used extensively and in a variety of dishes. In the nineteenth century in some districts, potatoes became a staple item in the peasant's diet.

If a peasant ate meat once a week—and then usually on Sundays—he was most fortunate. Generally, meat was associated with special celebrations. Most peasants considered the meat of bears, horses, and hares unfit for food, so that while these animals were plentiful they were rarely eaten. Fish was eaten wherever and whenever it was available.

Because most peasants had little money, it was a general maxim among them not to spend anything on themselves if they could possibly avoid doing so. As a result, almost all their food was grown on their own premises. Earthenware pots were the most common cooking utensils. Eating utensils were usually made of wood or pottery.

The most widespread peasant drink was *kvas,* a beer that was commonly made by pouring warm water on rye or barley and allowing it to ferment. Although tea was first introduced into Russia from China in the seventeenth century, it did not become a popular peasant drink until late in the nineteenth century. Subsequently, almost every peasant hut had its samovar to heat and hold hot water for tea. Tea was drunk regularly and often in large quantities. It was usually very weak and was served without milk. A common practice in drinking tea was to take a small lump of sugar between the teeth and let it melt as the tea was sipped.

The peasant was quite "proper" in his eating habits. He ate slowly and with, as one observer put it, "a great decorum." He crossed himself before and after each meal.

The peasant's dress was simple. In the summer, it consisted of a shirt of homespun tick or of chintz and trousers of light cotton or linen. A better-off peasant wore boots, but most of them wore bast shoes, which were common in Europe in the Middle Ages but had disappeared from use except in Russia among the peasants. In the winter, he wore a kind of homemade woolen boot and wrapped his legs with linen or cotton rags. His long homespun shirt was replaced by a sheepskin overcoat, which was worn by rich and poor alike. The peasant rarely took off this fur dress, often wearing it at night when he slept.

He tucked the bottom of his trousers into his boots. His shirt, however, was not tucked into his trousers but was worn outside. There was a saying in Russia at the time that so long as the Russian wore his shirt outside he was honest, but when he tucked it in, "like other Christians, he was no longer to be trusted."

He parted his hair in the middle and trimmed it in the shape of an inverted bowl. Usually, he did not trim his beard. On his head, he wore a cylindrical felt hat in summer and a fur or lambskin cap during the winter. In the nineteenth century, the visor cap came into use.

The basic dress of the female peasant was the *rubakha*, a knee-length shift quite similar in design and fabric to the man's shirt. In the summer, unmarried girls would wear this garment without any overgarment. Married women, however, almost always wore another garment over this shift. The woman's footwear was similar to the man's. In fact, among the poorer peasants, there was a great similarity in dress among men and women. On holidays, however, the women dressed in more colorful materials, with red, yellow, and blue predominating. Sometimes, dresses were embroidered and decorated with ribbons.

By the end of the nineteenth century and the beginning of the twentieth century, some of these customs of dress had changed somewhat, especially in those areas that were closer to cities. Clothes made from manufactured cloth instead of homespun were worn. One of the more common sights was the peddler, who went from village to village with a large pack on his back selling cloth and other items. He has been described as dressing "in a black frock-coat of an antiquated shape, a black waistcoat decorated with metal or glass buttons, black trousers and a cap with a black peak. Sometimes the man had a horse and cart to transport his goods, in which case he slowly walked the roads beside the horse. He had scarcely arrived in some hamlet when the whole population hurried out to meet him." There were no fixed prices on the goods, and a deal was made only after long and loud haggling.

There was a great deal of concern over the peasant woman's hair, and a number of customs reflected this concern. Like people almost everywhere and in almost all periods of time, the Russian peasant believed that hair, especially a woman's, was a strong sexual symbol and stimulant. An unmarried girl never cut her hair nor did she wear it loose in public. She braided it in a single plait, which she entwined with ribbons and other decorations at the time of various festivals. Only on her wedding day did she dare wear it loose in public. In the summer, she often wore a circlet with an open crown. Until the late eighteenth century, in winter she wore the same headgear as a man, but later she began to wear a kerchief on her head, often of bright colors. A married woman kept her head covered so that her hair was hidden, especially in the presence of strangers and, for modesty, in the presence of the older men of her husband's family.

Whether the appearance of the Russian peasant was pleasant or not depended on the eyes—and nose—of the observer. One writer described him thus:

"His hair and beard uncut and matted with the sweat and dirt of his toil; his tattered coat hanging from stooped shoulders; his legs swathed in woolen strips; his feet thrust into bast shoes— boots, if he were exceptionally prosperous—and his unwashed body giving acrid testimony of the chief elements in his daily monotonous routine—manure, earth, onions, cabbage."

However, Elizabeth Craven, an English noblewoman who visited Russia in the late eighteenth century, was pleasantly impressed by the Russian peasant. She noted that among the peasant girls, "some are beautiful, and do not look less so from various colored handkerchiefs tied over their forehead in a becoming and *pittoresque* manner." She found the Russian male peasant to be "a fine, stout, straight, well-looking man."

The "unwashed body" of the peasant was not, despite the foregoing quoted material, quite true to fact. In most peasant families, the weekly bath was almost a ritual. "Every family which is not totally destitute has its hot steam bath," wrote Stepniak, "where all wash . . . with great punctiliousness. The poorer among them, who have no bath of their own, use the family oven for this purpose, just after the removal of the coal. This is real martyrdom, as the first sensation of a man unaccustomed to such exploits is that of being roasted alive."

Almost all villages of any size had a *bania,* or bathhouse. There, peasants steamed and beat themselves with birch rods until they were, as one observer put it, "almost in a swoon." Most bathhouses had separate quarters for men and women.

The bania was a low, wooden building that contained a large brick stove. After the stove was heated, cold water was poured onto it so that the room soon became filled with steam. There were also boilers for hot water. A tier of benches was on one side of the room. If the peasant wished to soak himself in the hottest steam, he would lie on the highest tier of benches. The bath was a combination of steaming himself and washing away the perspiration with hot and then cold water while at various intervals he beat himself with birch rods or twigs. In winter, the more hearty peasants would rush out of the bathhouse—their naked bodies wet with perspiration and stinging from the beating with birch rods—and roll around in the snow.

The Russian peasant welcomed large families. The family bathhouse was a favorite spot for giving birth. The village midwife delivered the baby. If the infant was a male, its umbilical cord was cut with an axe, a symbol of masculinity. An infant girl's umbilical cord was cut with a distaff.

Babies were breast-fed. The pacifier often consisted of a tied rag containing bread or cooked groats. About three days after birth, the baby was christened either in the peasant's hut or at the village church. Babies were kept tightly swaddled in the belief that this gave them a feeling of security.

At the other end of man's life span, the peasant accepted death quite philosophically. Leo Tolstoy in his story "The Death of Ivan Ilyich" tried to show the kitchen peasant's understanding and compassion for those who were facing death. The Russian writer N. S. Leskov commented:

> Ivan Ilyich, deserted by everyone, having become a burden even to those closest to him, found real (in the spirit of the people) compassion and help only in his kitchen muzhik. . . . The master had himself

asked the peasant to come to him, and here before the open grave the kitchen muzhik had taught his master to appreciate genuine sympathy, which made what society people bring to each other at such times look insignificant and repugnant. . . . Ivan Ilyich had learned what can be learned from the kitchen muzhik, and—made healthy by that teaching—he died.

In the village among the peasants, there was an elaborate ritual when a member of the family was thought to be dying. The Orthodox priest was summoned to give the last rites. Traditionally and superstitiously, to end the peasant's suffering an opening often was made in the wall of the hut. After a peasant died, his body would be taken to a bench in the icon corner and positioned so that his head was near the icon and his feet toward the door. A candle was lit and placed in his hands, and he was then dressed in his best and placed in the coffin. In the coffin, too, the family placed an axe, a loaf of bread, and a lump of salt. The coffin was then carried out of the hut through a window, and care was taken that it not touch the framework so that no evil spirits would remain behind.

The coffin was then taken to the cemetery, where it was buried according to Orthodox rites. This was done just before sunset, so that, as one writer phrased it, "the sun can show Ivan's soul the way to his future abode in the dark beyond." After the funeral, the dead peasant's remaining clothes and bedding were burned. At the table that night, a place was left vacant for the dead man. His family then prayed for him on the ninth, twentieth, and fortieth days after his death, again six months after his death, and still again on various days noted on the church's calendar for prayers in memory of the dead.

Between life and death, the single most important personal event in the peasant's life was his marriage. However, there was very little romance or sentimentality about Russian peasant marriages. The wife was chosen because she would make a good worker, not because she would necessarily be an understanding and loving companion. This unromantic attitude fitted in well with the peasant's extremely practical and matter-of-fact conceptions and habits. He had no interest or desire to indulge himself in romantic or ethereal sentiments of any kind. Romantic love was simply not a part of his attitude toward women and especially not so in his search for a girl who would work hard, bear children, and obey his authority. In old Russia, it was rare among peasants that there was a so-called love match; almost all marriages were arranged by the parents of the boy and girl.

The job of getting a wife for a son was the responsibility of the peasant mother. In some villages, a matchmaker was used to mediate between the families of the intended bride and groom. Negotiations often concentrated on the size of the girl's dowry. This might involve how much linen, bedding, or even livestock the bride would bring to her marriage.

After an engagement had been agreed on, the girl was usually relieved of her housework so that she and her friends could prepare certain linens and other items for her dowry. The girl was supposed to look sad from this time on until her marriage, in accordance with the Russian proverb: "Weeping bride, laughing wife: laughing bride, weeping wife."

The night before the wedding, the bride and her friends took a ritual bath and the groom brought gifts to the home of his bride. Then, he and his friends had a bachelor party at his house while the girl spent her "last night of maidenhood" with her friends at her house.

On the wedding day, there were many rituals that each performed in their respective homes, including the unbraiding of the girl's hair and the blessing of the boy with the family icon. At the church, they were wed in the Orthodox ceremony, after which the girl's hair was braided, fastened to her head, and crowned with the married woman's headdress.

The married couple, their families, and friends then went to the home of the groom for the ceremonial welcoming and blessing with hops and kernels of grain. The groom's father removed the bride's veil, and the family and guests then began eating and drinking. The bride and groom ate separately at another table until they were finally led to the main table to join the others. The bride then took off her husband's boots as a sign of her submission to him.

When the feasting was over, the bride and groom were led to their bed and the guests sang suggestive songs about the events that were to transpire that night with the newlyweds. The next morning, the bride's shift was examined, and if it was spotted with blood that was proof that she was, indeed, a virgin. To the beating of pots and pans, the shift was then paraded around the room for all to see. The couple were then taken to the bathhouse, and together they took their ritual steam bath.

For the next two days, there were various feasts, dances, and games. Finally, the festivities were over, and the bride began her married life in the hut of her husband's parents. Eventually, if there were no offspring, the marriage could be annulled.

Adultery was not uncommon, and when it occurred it was a source of much gossip in the village. A typical peasant proverb dealing with adultery was that "the devil pours a spoonful of honey into someone else's wife." Families not directly involved did not interfere; it was considered the husband's duty to punish his wife's misconduct. If the wife was not a good worker, sometimes he would use this as an excuse to get her out of his house. If she was a good worker, he gave her a good beating and instructed his mother to keep her so busy that she would have no time for other men. In the typical peasant household, the mother-in-law was only too happy to oblige.

10 The Peasant Character

To delineate the Russian peasant's character accurately is a task that almost every great writer of Russia has set for himself. The result has been that each writer—as well as each non-literary observer—has seen the peasant as he wanted to see him: according to his own class upbringing, religious and moral beliefs, and political goals. Although certain outstanding characteristics could be—and were—described, what did they all add up to in the making of a man? How does one reconcile a whole series of conflicting characteristics, each of which was part of the actions, thoughts, and very soul of the peasant? How true to his basic character are the outward manifestations of an oppressed man when he lives in constant fear of beatings, hunger, homelessness, and political oppression? What reveals the true character of a man—what he does and what he says, or what he does not do and what he does not say, or both?

These questions—and many more—can be frustratingly applied

to the Russian peasant in relation to his character. However, the life and history of the peasant can be described with some degree of general agreement. For instance, few persons would too seriously disagree with Soviet writer Boris Pilniak's somewhat cynical description of the peasant existence. He wrote: "Peasant life is known. It is to eat in order to work, to work in order to eat and, besides that, to be born, to bear, and to die."

The peasant was superstitious and believed in a wide variety of mysterious signs and portents, yet he was earthy and matter-of-fact. He was extremely pious, religious, and kind, yet he was capable of diabolically cruel behavior. He was tolerant of despotism, yet he was stubborn and, at times, rebellious against those who oppressed him. He was obedient almost to the point of servility, yet he could be unyielding if he believed he had been wronged. He could be one of the most humane of individuals, yet he was often vicious to those closest to him.

In trying to find answers to these contradictions, persons have talked about the "Russian soul" or the "mystical relationship of the peasant to the earth."

Dostoevsky, who spent a good deal of time in a Siberian prison with a number of peasants, viewed them as embodying the highest national and universal human truths.

Tolstoy—who was constantly torn between the life of action and the life of thought, between the life of a landowner and the life of a sacrificing reformer—was greatly drawn to the peasant. He saw the peasant's life as simple and good, and his view of man and God as untarnished by intellectualism. Here, indeed, was the pure man who could teach everyone the meaning of life.

Unlike Dostoevsky and Tolstoy, Turgenev did not stress the spiritual or universal values of the peasant. He saw him as a many-faceted human being who went about his day-to-day affairs like any other individual.

Chekhov, with his gentle but powerfully realistic and discerning eye, saw the peasant as a victim of life and history and not as a teacher of anyone. He viewed him as an equal citizen in an unequal society. One of the characters in his play *The Cherry Orchard* says:

In the course of the summer and winter there had been hours and days when it had seemed that these people lived worse than cattle, when it had been terrible to live with them; they were coarse, not honest; filthy, not sober; they lived in discord, quarreling constantly, because they did not respect but feared and suspected one another. Who keeps the tavern, makes the people drunkards? A peasant. Who embezzles and drinks up the communal school and church funds? A peasant. Who has stolen from his neighbor, committed arson, given false testimony in court for a bottle of vodka? Who at *zemstvo* [the elective district or provincial administrative assembly] and other meetings is the first to declaim against the peasants? A peasant. Yes, to live with them was terrible, yet all the same they were people; they suffered and wept as people do; and in their lives there was nothing for which excuse might not be found.

Gorky, whose early life was spent close to the peasant, had the least sympathy or respect for him. He saw him as the depraved product of a depraved society. He viewed him as mean and cunning, like an animal that had to have these characteristics in order to exist in a hostile and bitter world. He felt he had no meaningful traditions or great heroes and that his only accomplishments were the development of cynicism and cruelty.

In 1922, five years after the revolution, Gorky wrote: "Where, then, is that good-natured, thoughtful, Russian peasant, that tireless seeker after truth and justice, about whom Russian literature of the nineteenth century told the world so convincingly and beautifully? In my youth, I sought diligently for such a man through the villages of Russia—and did not find him."

The writer Gleb Uspensky's description of the peasant was blunt and devoid of romanticism or nationalism. His views approached the sociological, somewhat scientific analysis that started to be fashionable in the early twentieth century. He wrote:

In the tiller of the soil there is not a step, not an action, not a thought which does not belong to the earth. He is in complete bondage to the little green blade of grass. To such an extent is it impossible for him to tear himself free from this power, that when he is asked, "What do you want, imprisonment or flogging?" he will always prefer to be flogged, to suffer physical torture, only in order that he may be immediately free—because his master, the earth, will not wait: the mowing must be done, the cattle needs hay, the earth needs cattle. . . .

He is not responsible for a thing, not for a single step he takes. Once he acts as his mistress, the earth, commands, he is answerable for nothing. He has killed a man who was stealing his horse—and is guiltless, since without the horse he cannot work the land. All his children have died—again, he is not at fault; the land did not bring forth, there was nothing to feed them with. He has driven this wife of his into the grave —and is innocent: she, the fool, was a poor housekeeper and lazy; through her the whole thing, the work, came to a standstill. And their mistress, the earth, demands this work; it will not wait. In a word, if he only heeds what the earth commands, he is guiltless in everything; and the main thing is—what happiness not to be inventing a life for oneself, not to be seeking for interests and sensations, since they appear of themselves every day, as soon as you have opened your eyes! If it's raining outside—you must sit at home; if it's a warm, dry day, you must go mowing, harvesting, etc. Responsible for nothing, devising nothing himself, a man lives only by obeying, and that obedience—every minute, every second—when expressed in constant work, forms a life that has no apparent result (what they earn they consume), but that has a result precisely in itself.

One of the outstanding peasant characteristics was obedience to authority, whether it was his master, his state official, or his czar. "The power of the land," the writer John Maynard claimed, "and of all those institutions of the commune inseparably bound up with the power of the land, crushed him relentlessly, unless he yielded an absolute obedience."

From his earliest childhood, the peasant was brought up to obey. First, it was obedience to his father. Then, to his commune and to his master. And throughout his life, to the state.

One commentator pointed out that in the early underground work against the czar, a peasant worker approached a Communist leader and offered his help, saying, "When I was a boy I obeyed my father, and since I have begun to work I have obeyed my master, and now I am going to obey you. You know what to do and I don't. Just tell me." The commentator further observed that "lacking any abstract notion of institutionalized power, the peasant was loyal to God rather than to the church, to the czar rather than to the imperial government, (and later), to Stalin rather than to the party."

This obedience could have had its origin, in part, as Dostoevsky believed, in the peasant being dominated by the "stream of suffering" that existed throughout his history. This may have given rise to a kind of fatalism that many peasants evidenced. For example, a peasant mother, upon the impending death of her daughter, was said to have remarked resignedly: "She will die; and there will be less cost."

Obedience, resignation, and fatalism were accompanied by a remarkable stoicism. The peasant seemed to be unconcerned with material comforts. He was spartan in his indifference to hardship and often felt that this was an attribute of man's strength and fortitude. Uncomplainingly, for example, he could stand extremes of heat and cold and even delighted in the rapid transition from one extreme to another as when he went in the winter from the excessive heat of the bathhouse to roll around in the freezing snow outside.

In the army, the peasant soldier was known for his acceptance of privation, disease, and death without complaint, his ability to subsist on meager rations, and his willingness to undergo the most severe climatic hardships.

Still, he could be—and often was—defiant and even rebellious. Like oppressed people in many other countries, he expressed his defiance in song. Here is one nineteenth-century song of defiance:

> He has destroyed us,
>   The evil *barin*, the seignior.
> It was he, the evil one, who chose
>   The young men,
> The young men,
>   To be soldiers,
> And us, the beautiful girls,
>   To be servants;
> The young married women
>   To suckle his children,
> And our fathers and mothers
>   For labor.
> But our young men gathered
>   On the steep hill—
> Our young men defied
>   The lord-barin:
> Seignior, author of evil,

We will not be soldiers for you;
The beautiful girls
    Shall not be your servants,
The young mothers
    Shall not nurse your children,
And the fathers and mothers
    Shall labor for you no more.

Another form of protest was petitioning the government for redress of wrongdoing on the part of their masters or government officials. The filing of petitions was forbidden by law, and there were severe penalties levied against those persons who circumvented their masters and appealed directly to the government for assistance. Nevertheless, petitions were circulated and forwarded to government agencies.

Still another mode of defiance was flight from the estates of their masters. Under serfdom this was a crime, and the peasant could be severely punished. Yet tens of thousands of serfs made their way to distant parts, especially to Siberia.

More violent forms of defiance sometimes involved burning down the estate houses of their masters, stealing the animals, killing the master and his family, and then running away to be fugitives from the law. These acts of defiance, in some cases, became small-scale uprisings. Between 1774 and 1796, there were twenty such uprisings recorded in the state archives, although most historians believe that the actual number was larger. In the brief reign of Paul I (1796–1801), 278 disturbances were reported in thirty-two provinces.

Although most of these uprisings were on a small scale, there were several large-scale, widespread peasant revolts, notably those led by Stenka Razin, Kondratii Bulavin, and Emelian Pugachev.

The earliest of these was the 1670–71 uprising of the peasants in the Volga basin, led by a Cossack of the Don, Stenka Razin. Razin called on the peasants to revolt against their masters, promising them freedom and a better life, and thousands of peasants joined his band. The rebels took control of the region of the Don, attacked and sacked the Volga town of Tsaritsyn (modern-day Volgograd, formerly Stalingrad), and continued north along the Volga River, looting and burning. The revolt encompassed a broad area—from Astrakhan to the vicinity of Nizhni Novgorod (now the city of Gorki), 250 miles from Moscow. Razin's forces were defeated by the government at the fortress of Simbirsk. Subsequently, he was turned over to the government by the ataman of the Don Cossacks and sent to Moscow, where he underwent unbelievable torture and was executed in Red Square in June, 1671.

In 1707, another revolt broke out among the Don Cossacks, this one led by Kondratii Bulavin. His proclamations and appeals to the peasants, like those of Razin, promised freedom and a better life. Again, thousands of peasants heeded his appeal. The following year, his forces were defeated, and his followers were severely punished by torture and execution. Bulavin himself committed suicide.

The most serious rebellion was that of Emelian Pugachev in 1773. He rallied the Cossacks from the River Iaik and a number of members of the religious sect, the Old Believers. He declared himself to be the deceased Czar Peter III, vowed he would shut up the then-reigning Czarina Catherine II (the Great) in a nunnery, and began his march to Moscow. Pugachev was joined by thousands of Cossacks from the Don and by large numbers of non-Russians—including Tatars, Kirghiz, Bashkirs, Mordvins, Chuvashes, Votyaks, and Finns.

He issued proclamations of a truly revolutionary nature, promising his followers and the peasants of Russia freedom and the ownership of the land. Pugachev captured town after town along the Volga and in the Urals. As the rebellion progressed, it became more and more a peasant war against the government. Hundreds of priests and government officials were hanged and estates of the landlords were burned and plundered. For a while, officials in Moscow feared that Pugachev and his peasant army would, indeed, reach Moscow and take over the government.

On July 31, 1774, Pugachev issued a manifesto to the serfs in the region he then occupied. It proclaimed that henceforth they were free from their serfdom and from all duties and obligations to their masters and the state. He gave them ownership of "the fields, forests, meadows, fisheries, and saltpans without cost and without obrok." He ordered them to exterminate the landlords, calling them "the foes of our rule and the disturbers of the empire and the despoilers of the peasants." He promised them that after the nobles were killed, "everyone will be able to enjoy tranquility and a peaceful life that will endure till the end of time." Tens of thousands of serfs heeded his appeal, left their villages, and joined his army.

For a time, there was a frantic flight of landlords from their estates to the cities, even to Moscow. The peasants hunted the nobles down and killed them. Gibbets were raised wherever the rebels marched, and hundreds of persons were put to death. "In some villages," reported a government official, "these murders have so completely exterminated the proprietorial families that it is not yet known to whom the villages ought legally to pass."

One government expedition after another was defeated by the rebels. Finally, however, Pugachev's poorly equipped catch-all army was defeated decisively near Tsaritsyn, and his followers began to disband. Pugachev fled to the steppes, was betrayed by his own followers, and was brought in an iron cage to Moscow. He was executed there in January 1775.

In some respects, the cruelty and callousness shown by the peasants to their masters during various uprisings showed that they had learned well from the centuries of cruelty and oppression on the part of their masters. Yet the peasant could be—and was—cruel to his own. Sometimes it was a result of his deep frustration and sometimes it seemed to be part of his approach to life.

The peasant was also good-natured and affectionate. Wallace, who observed them carefully, wrote:

> No class of men in the world is more good-natured and pacific than the Russian peasantry. When sober they never fight, and even when under the influence of alcohol they are more likely to be violently affectionate than disagreeably quarrelsome. If two of them take to drinking together, the probability is that in a few minutes, though they may never have seen each other before, they will be expressing in very strong terms their mutual regard and affection, confirming their words with an occasional friendly embrace.

Few observers have regarded the peasant as dignified. Usually, the peasant has been viewed as being obsequious to those who had power over him. Stepniak, however, tried to explain that this obsequiousness was really a kind of dignity.

"It stands to reason," Stepniak wrote, "that the ideas of personal dignity held by our muzhiks are not the same as those held by the people of the civilized countries of Europe. When meeting 'a gentleman' or an official, no matter of what grade, the peasant will take off his hat and stand bareheaded when spoken to. If anxious to express extreme gratitude to anyone, he may perchance bow down to the ground, as grown-up children bowed to their parents in the families of the middle classes up to the present generation. The muzhiks do not consider any of these acts to be humiliating, holding still in this respect to the same standards or ideas as have prevailed in all countries, modern and ancient, when just emerging from the patriarchal state."

If there was some doubt as to whether or not the peasant had dignity, there was no doubt at all that the peasant had few rivals in his Homeric style of drinking. The poet N. A. Nekrasov observed in the 1870s that the peasant is "working himself to death and half-killing himself with drink." According to established custom, scarcely a single event in the life of the community was celebrated without the drinking of vodka, whether it was the cutting of hay or the observance of a local saint's day. Likewise, almost all events in the family were celebrated with vodka—births, marriages, funeral feasts, and going into the army.

The government did nothing to discourage drinking, since the sale of spirits was a government monopoly that produced a huge revenue. The Englishman Giles Fletcher reported that a wife or child was forbidden to go into a tavern and urge the peasant to go home. "None may call them foorth," wrote Fletcher in the late sixteenth century, "whatsoever cause there be, because he hindereth the emperour's revenue."

Drinking was heaviest on Sundays and holidays. As a rule, the peasant didn't drink constantly but, as one observer noted, "in huge spurts." Women drank as much and as often as the men and boasted of their prowess in this area. Lady Craven, in fact, wondered if "it is a religious duty for the Russian peasant to be drunk."

Just before the Revolution of 1917, the American writer Ernest
Poole visited Russia, and in his account of his journey he reported
on a conversation he had with a peasant, who recounted the drunkenness in his village. The peasant said:

> When I was a child, over half the peasants would be drunk for days
> at a time. There were fights along the river front. . . . And this was
> nothing uncommon. Things had gone from bad to worse—till a bottle
> of vodka came to be used as a standard unit of value. When a peasant
> was asked what a job would cost, he would answer not in rubles, but
> in bottles of vodka. If there was none to be had in the stores, the peas-
> ants would refuse to work; but when it came, there would be a rush
> to earn money to buy drink. Merchants from the large towns came
> here with carts and wagons loaded down with vodka, and for this the
> half-crazed people parted with their grain, their cows, their very last
> belongings.
>
> As the women began to drink with the men, it caused a sex prom-
> iscuity that spread disease at a fearful rate. Many children were born
> idiots. In the village down by the river where we went the other night,
> there were almost always men and women and boys lying drunk in
> the ditches.
>
> In the winter, every week or two, you would hear of some drunk-
> ard frozen to death. And once, when a river merchant got married
> and at his wedding the vodka flowed free, forty-six peasants lost their
> lives—for winter is no child's play here and one must not fall asleep on
> the snow.
>
> After a Russian holiday, nearly every peasant's wife would have a
> black eye or a bruise. There was a saying among them: "He has been
> drunk from sunrise." Toward night I could hear them coming home,
> men and women, singing and howling like gray wolves. . . .
>
> You often saw children drunk as well. Many of the mothers put
> vodka into their babies' milk. "It is good for my baby," one woman
> told me. "See how well it makes him sleep." Often a peasant mother
> would chew a mouthful of black bread, then take it out and soak it in
> vodka and so give it to her child.
>
> I remember seeing men in those days who went about wearing
> nothing but their shirts. They had sold or pawned the rest of their
> clothes. And half-naked women, too, were by no means uncommon
> sights. Anything for alcohol. . . .

Accounts vary as to the honesty of the peasant. For instance,
Haxthausen reported that the peasant paid his taxes honestly and
promptly:

There is scarcely an instance recorded of any collectors of the crown taxes, who traverse the country with considerable sums of money, being attacked and robbed. . . . When a collector enters a village, he taps at each window and calls out, "*Kaza!*" Then each person brings out his crown tax for the year and throws it into the open bag: the collector does not count the money, being well assured that he is never cheated. If his visit is in the night, he enters the first substantial house, places the moneybag under the image of the saint, looks for a place to rest on, and sleeps with perfect assurance of finding his money safe in the morning.

Wallace, on the other hand, reported that when he was in Russia and traveling at night, he

> discovered on awaking that my driver was bending over me, and had introduced his hand into one of my pockets; but the incident ended without serious consequences. When I caught the delinquent hand, and demanded an explanation from the owner, he replied, in an apologetic, caressing tone, that the night was cold, and he wished to warm his fingers; and when I advised him to use for that purpose his own pockets rather than mine, he promised to act in the future according to my advice.

Wallace also noted, however, that among themselves the Russians were, as a rule, "not addicted to thieving, as is proved by the fact that they often leave their doors unlocked when all the inmates of the houses are in the fields; but if the muzhik finds in the proprietor's farmyard a piece of iron, or a bit of rope, or any of those things which he constantly requires and has great difficulty in obtaining, he is very apt to pick it up and carry it home. His notions of property with regard to such articles are very similar to those of servants in many other countries with regard to eatables."

Likewise, there is a difference of opinion regarding the inclination of the Russian peasant to lie. Dostoevsky saw a propensity toward lying in the peasant, and in Russians in general. In his *Diary of a Writer*, Dostoevsky asks, "Why does everyone in Russia lie and without exception?" He then answers his question by noting that the Russians "lie out of hospitality," with "the most honorable purposes," and "for the purpose of creating an esthetic impression upon the hearer." The Russians, he wrote, "fear the truth, that is, we do not fear it, if you wish, but constantly regard the truth as something far too tedious and prosaic, insufficiently poetic, too commonplace, and in this way, by constantly avoiding it, we finally made it one of the most unusual and rare things in the Russian world."

Wallace said of the Russian peasants:

> When dealing with the authorities, [they] consider the most patent and barefaced falsehoods as a fair means of self-defense. Thus, for example, when a muzhik is implicated in a criminal affair, and a preliminary investigation is being made, he probably begins by constructing an elaborate story to explain the facts and exculpate himself. The story may be a tissue of self-evident falsehoods from beginning to end, but he defends it valiantly as long as possible. When he perceives that the position which he has taken up is utterly untenable, he declares openly that all he has said is false, and that he wishes to make a new declaration. This second declaration may have the same fate as the former one, and then he proposes a third. Thus groping his way, he tries various stories till he finds one that seems proof against all objections. In the fact of his thus telling lies there is of course nothing remarkable, for criminals in all parts of the world have a tendency to deviate from the truth when they fall into the hands of justice. The peculiarity is that he retracts his statements with the composed air of a chess-player who requests his opponent to let him take back an inadvertent move.

The laziness of the peasant has been commented on by most observers of Russian peasant life. That he was no dynamo in his everyday actions was quite obvious to all. Whether he was unique in this regard in Russian society is doubtful. The nobles were certainly not models of energy, and their indolence has been reported in numerous Russian novels and plays. The government bureaucrat, who has been described as "devoting the entire morning in his office to the smoking of cigarettes," was also far from the energetic counterpart of the indolent peasant. In old Russia, then, the laziness of the peasant was certainly not unique. At least, he had an excuse for indolence, as the English traveler Richardson pointed out in the 1760s:

> As a Russian peasant has no property, can enjoy none of the fruits of his own labour more than is sufficient to preserve his existence, and can transmit nothing to his children but the inheritance of wretched

bondage, he thinks of nothing beyond the present. You are not, of consequence, to expect among them much industry and exertion. Exposed to corporal punishment, and put on the footing of irrational animals, how can they possess the spirit and elevation of sentiment which distinguish the natives of a free state? Treated with so much inhumanity, how can they be humane? I am confident that most of the defects which appear in their national character are in consequence of the despotism of the Russian government.

11 Religion, the Church, and Superstition

A RUSSIAN peasant was often called a *krest'ianin,* which means "Christian," "human being in general," and "tax-paying villager." These meanings incorporate a number of fundamental aspects of the peasant—his religion, his humanity, and his economic status. The word "krest'ianin" was in common use in old Russia. In certain regions and in certain periods of time, it was used as frequently as the word "muzhik."

Outwardly, by word and sign, the peasant was extremely religious. He called upon God in dozens of various verbal expressions and crossed himself at all the appropriate occasions. Nevertheless, just how deep was his piety and how fervent was his religious zeal are debatable.

One observer believed that the peasant had the deepest, truest kind of religion because he involved himself with "the most important problems that can concern the human soul—truth and untruth, Christ and Antichrist, eternity, man, salvation." The Russian writer Gogol insisted that the Russian people and especially the peasants were the most religious people in the world. Chekhov observed that they tenderly and reverently loved the Scriptures. An early nineteenth-century observer wrote that "religion in one form or another seemed to be constantly in the thoughts of peasants." The writer Maurice Baring insisted that "anybody who gets to know the Russian people at all well, will be struck by the unmistakable evidence of inward religious feeling which they display."

Stepniak, on the other hand, made little of the fact that the peasant was constantly uttering God's name on every conceivable occasion and prostrating himself fervently before icons. He felt that, except for members of certain religious splinter groups such as the Old Believers, the Russian peasant was not genuinely religious. D. Mackenzie Wallace observed much the same thing and wrote:

> It must be admitted that the Russian people are in a certain sense religious. They go regularly to church on Sundays and holy days, cross themselves repeatedly when they pass a church or icon, take the Holy Communion at stated seasons, rigorously abstain from animal food—not only on Wednesdays and Fridays, but also during Lent and the other long fasts—make occasional pilgrimages to holy shrines, and, in a word, fulfill punctiliously the ceremonial observance which they suppose necessary for salvation. But here their religiousness ends. They are generally profoundly ignorant of religious doctrine, and know little or nothing of Holy Writ.

The peasants were linked with the church almost exclusively through the village clergy. By and large, the village clergy was a poverty-ridden group. In many cases, there was little economic distinction between the village priest and the village peasant. An early eighteenth-century writer observed: "Among us in Russia the village priests support themselves by their own labor, and are in no way distinguishable from the peasants who till the soil; the muzhik is at the plough, the priest is at the plough; the muzhik is at the scythe, the priest is at the scythe; and the holy church and pastoral care are neglected."

The village priest supplemented his income by small fees he received from the peasants for performing various religious ceremonies. But even these pittances—sometimes only a few kopecks

—were often the cause of bitter haggling between himself and his parishioners. In addition, he also had his church superiors and the state to contend with, each demanding a portion of the meager income he received for the various religious ceremonies he performed.

The morals and morality of the village priest often were not above suspicion. Like the peasants, he was a heavy drinker. Sometimes, he was the village drunkard. He was not averse to indulging in adventures with women. Oftentimes, he was the object of scorn or amusement to the villagers, rather than the respected leader of a flock of the faithful. One confidential report to the government on the state of the clergy in Nizhni Novgorod province noted:

"Can the people respect the clergy when they hear how one priest stole money from below the pillow of a dying man at the moment of confession? How another was publicly dragged out of a house of ill-fame? How a third christened a dog? How a fourth whilst officiating at an Easter service was dragged by the hair from the altar by the deacon?"

Actually, the village priest was neither angel nor devil. Usually, he was himself a peasant with a peasant upbringing, and his manner of life did not completely change once he became a priest. He often lived in the same village where he was raised. He had as much—or as little—to eat as before. And he tilled the land in the same way as his parishioners. His house was often no larger, neater, or newer than a peasant's. His wife—in the Orthodox faith nonmonastic priests were permitted to marry—was a peasant, too, and behaved like one. Her only advantage, perhaps, was that she was usually treated better by her husband than was the typical peasant wife. Since a priest was allowed to marry only once, the number of beatings she received were minimal, and he paid more attention than did most peasants to his wife's health and well-being.

The variations in the "goodness" of priests and their general character and makeup were noted by H. W. Williams, who observed them shortly before the Russian revolution. He wrote:

> Sometimes priests are hopelessly ignorant and stupid, and hold their position in spite of obvious incapacity only through the protec-

tion of powerful relatives. Sometimes they give way to drink. . . . The average priest is neither conspicuously devout nor conspicuously negligent. He is a hearty fellow with a broad accent, rather overburdened by the cares of his office and by family cares, not keenly intelligent, but shrewd, observant, with common sense and humour. He is not interested in theoretical questions, is sincere in his religious beliefs, takes the world as he finds it, and feels thoroughly at home in it, and able to enjoy its good things when they come to him. . . . There are not a few priests who delight in their office, who are full of a warm and simple faith, and who toil in poor parishes all their lives long without any other object than that of doing good. The wonder, considering all the conditions of service, is not that there are so few good priests, but that there are so many of them.

The peasant did not judge his village priest too harshly. He viewed him first as a human being, and then as his priest. And he saw him, too, as having all the weaknesses of other human beings. As Wright Williams observed:

The peasant, to judge by all accounts, regarded the priest or "pope" as in daily life somewhat less than a whole man, but as the necessary personage for births, weddings, funerals, and a few other occasions. Ceremonial observance was more important than doctrine, and the wrestlings of individual conscience mattered less than the sharing in the community life of the church services, where there was something of the same feeling of brotherhood as in the gatherings of the mir, which settled so many secular problems for you, no one knew quite how.

It is doubtful if the parish priests had a great hold on the peasants, except in their insistence that they practice the various rituals and observances. With their masters, their government, and their mir all exercising one form or another of control, the church and its priests just didn't matter that much in the affairs that meant most to the peasants—their land, their food, their homes, and their families.

It has been estimated that at the turn of the nineteenth century about 13 million Eastern Slavs (approximately 15 percent) were members of one dissident religious group or another. Generally, these sects were composed overwhelmingly of peasants. They were characterized as having leaders who were morally inspiring but intellectually weak. Most of the leaders had little education or were completely illiterate. They were often superstitious but had a frenzied attachment to their particular belief.

In the main, the sects fell into two groups. One group, such as the Old Believers, considered themselves to be the only really true followers of Orthodoxy. The other developed their own beliefs and did not consider themselves to be an offshoot of Orthodoxy, or their beliefs as being based on its doctrine or ritual. Some of the dissident groups had an anticzarist, antigovernment, and antiserfdom attitude.

The largest group by far was the Old Believers. They had their origin in the seventeenth century, when they objected to the official gospel as interpreted by the then-reigning leader of the Russian Orthodox Church, Patriarch Nikhon. The original leaders of the Old Believers were four dissident Orthodox priests—Avvakum, Feodor, Lazar, and Epifany, who for ten years preached against Nikhon's reforms. They were condemned by the Council of 1666–67 and in 1682 were burned at the stake.

The doctrines of the Old Believers forbade them to frequent the established church, to prostrate themselves before holy images, or to use incense or candles. They insisted on crossing themselves with two fingers instead of three. They believed that the reforms of Nikhon were not only wrong in themselves but that such innovations were a portent of the coming of the Antichrist and the nearness of the Apocalypse. With few exceptions, most of the leaders were devout semiliterates and illiterates. Their followers repeated a theology that was based on half-understood memorized passages in the Scriptures. They were extremely zealous in their faith and were willing to undergo any oppression and condemnation in order to keep their faith and beliefs. They were one of the groups that were against Westernization and serfdom.

Dostoevsky, who was imprisoned in Siberia together with several Old Believers, wrote about them in his book *The House of the Dead,* an account of his years in prison. "They were highly developed people . . . shrewd peasants, believing pedantically and uncritically in the literal truth of their old books."

Some of the other sects included the *Dukhobory* (Spirit-Wrestlers), the *Molokane* (Milk-Drinkers), the *Khlysty* (Flagellants), and the *Skoptsy* (Eunuchs). The first two were among those sects that condemned serfdom. Some members of the Dukhobory practiced collectivism and maintained common flocks, herds, and granaries, and distributed their crops to each member "according to his needs." One group among the Molokane established communes in the Caucasus and in eastern Siberia. These two sects as well as the Khlysty did not forbid conjugal union but did repudiate the sacrament of matrimony. The Skoptsy engaged in the mutilation of the sex organs of both men and women in order to make sexual intercourse impossible. The Skoptsy practiced mutilation not only on adults but on children, too. Sometimes, members refused to practice mutilation—castration, for example—and sometimes they were penalized by the group for bearing children.

The Khlysty engaged not only in the reading of the Bible and in sermonizing but also had secret rites for the initiated, presided over by a woman assistant known as the "prophetess" or "Mother of God." Many of their meetings were held at night. They started off with readings from the Bible and singing of hymns. They then had dances that became increasingly more violent, inducing hysteria and trances. Sometimes, the meetings ended, it was rumored, in rites that included mass acts of sexual intercourse. It was this group to which Grigori Rasputin, the adviser to the last czar and czarina of Russia, was accused of belonging. He was investigated and cleared of the charge.

The Dukhobory and Molokane often suffered imprisonment and exile for their anticzarist and antigovernment beliefs and practices. In one of their confessions in 1791, a Dukhobory group said: "Verily the children of God have no need either of czars or ruling powers or of any human laws whatever." Sometimes, they refused to pay their taxes and at other times refused to be inducted into the army. And, during the Crimean War, the Molokane were said to have offered prayers for the defeat of the Russian government, which was persecuting them.

In 1842, the government classified the various dissident groups as the less pernicious (those who accepted priests), the pernicious (the more moderate of the priestless groups), and the most pernicious (those who repudiated marriage and refused to pray for the

czar, as well as all the Dukhobory and Molokane sects). The first
two classifications the government hoped to keep in check; the
third classification it hoped to destroy. The program was not successful; by the middle of the century there were still about eight
million members of these sects out of a total population of about
sixty-nine million.

The Russians were not converted to Christianity until the very
end of the tenth century, and many of them had what amounted
to a duality of belief—the Christian and the pagan. Side by side
with his religion, the peasant believed in a host of superstitions.
The Russian peasant was not unique in being superstitious, for
superstitious people were found everywhere. This was especially
true among those living close to the land and whose lives were
governed to a large extent by the forces of nature. For instance,
Russian peasant sheds were hung with various kinds of charms to
guard domestic animals from harm. On their huts, they had a cross
crudely scrawled in red or white paint to keep away evil spirits.

The peasant's life was peopled with a host of spirits and sorcerers. There were the *leshii*, spirits who lived in the forests and
had a bluish skin, protruding eyes, and long hair. It was this spirit
who protected criminals and wrongdoers. He imitated birdsongs,
made weird mocking sounds in the forests, and laughed violently.
He was a great prankster and often led people astray in the forests.
Ways of countering his tricks were to wear one's jacket back to
front or to wear the left shoe on the right foot and the right shoe
on the left foot. Among peasants who lived on the steppes, the
counterpart of the leshii was the *polevik*.

The *vodyanoi*, the spirit of the waters, was old and ugly and
had a green beard. When he was feeling good, he guided the fish
into the peasant's net, but when he was feeling mean, he tore the
nets, raised storms, and upset the boats. When he was in a rage or
drunk, he caused floods and broke dikes. In the waters, too, were
the *rusalki*, water sprites, lovely naked girls with skin the color of
moonlight, silken hair, and emerald eyes. By their beauty, laughter,
and song, they enticed men into dangerous waters, where they
drowned.

The *vedmi*, witches or sorcerers, were wicked, toothless old women who practiced black magic. They rode on brooms at night and cast evil spells on people. The *baba-yaga* was a hideously ugly, hook-nosed creature—a witch who traveled about the countryside. She sat on a mortar, holding a pestle in her right hand to force her way and a broom in her left hand to wipe away the signs of her passage. She lived in a windowless, doorless mobile hut that was mounted on chicken's feet. A hideous black cat lived in the yard.

A number of spirits lived inside the peasant's house—in the chimney, under the floor, on the beams. The "leader" of the household spirits was the *domovoi*. He was old and slovenly. His body was hairy and he had a tail. He protected the family, shared in its life, settled arguments, and cured the sick. He was also full of pranks and deviltry. He made people snore, tangled a woman's hair, hid the master's boots, upset the chickens, and broke a leg of a bench. He had companions in the farmyard, the *dvorovoi;* in the stable, the *konyushennik;* and in the bathhouse, the *bannik.* With their naked backs to the half-open door of the bathhouse, girls would question the bannik about their future. This usually occurred around midnight. If the bannik scratched them, it was a bad sign for their future happiness; if he caressed them, they could expect the best.

In addition to these spirits of the forests, plains, waters, and hearth, there were the spirits of the dead, who returned to aid or plague the living. The *tchur,* or dead ancestor, had the privilege of demanding veneration. The practice of taking burning coals from the hearth of an old home to that of a new one symbolized the passing of the spirits of the ancestors from one dwelling to another.

These pagan beliefs and customs were enhanced by a large number of folk songs and folk tales that frequently embodied both Christianity and paganism. Few members of the nobility or merchant class believed in these pagan spirits and customs. The peasants were one with the nobles in their belief in Orthodoxy, but they parted company with them in the duality of belief. In a sense, the peasants had their own "City of God" in which they felt secure and comfortable and from which the landlords were excluded.

12 Flight and Migration

THE peasantry was not strictly an agricultural group. It was actually a group with three different but interrelated parts. It was village-based and agricultural; it was nomadic, with the peasants working in several areas—agriculture, forestry, fishing, crafts, and manufacturing—and it was city-based, with peasants engaged in a wide variety of jobs in large towns and cities—factory workers, cab drivers, street laborers, and servants. Thus, the peasantry was both stationary and mobile.

The stationary status of the agricultural peasants was for both legal and administrative reasons. Beginning with the decrees of Czar Peter I, the peasant was tied to the master's estate as the master's property. Administratively, the government knew where each "soul" was and could collect its soul tax.

The peasant's mobility arose from historic and economic causes. For centuries, the peasant had migrated from one area to another to improve his economic status or to escape oppression. During the Tatar domination from the thirteenth to the fifteenth century, the peasant moved freely from manor to manor. In Ivan the Terrible's reign in the sixteenth century, the peasant began to migrate to the great new colonial regions that were being opened by conquest in eastern European Russia and in Siberia. Subsequently, peasants continued to find new opportunities in one or another area of this vast empire, many of them joining nomadic Cossack bands. Some peasants ran away from their masters for economic reasons and others to escape from their cruelty. Still others went to the freer areas of the great Russian frontier to avoid conscription into the army or to be free of the autocratic police-state policies of the czarist government.

Some authorities claim that, in the nineteenth century, as many as six million peasants each year were on the move. In one instance, Haxthausen reported a commune was so depopulated by temporarily migrating peasants that of the 9,500 male souls on the Revision lists, 7,000 were "go-aways." During their absence, the peasants were still retained on the Revision lists and kept their communal rights.

Throughout Russia, peasants could be seen going from one place to another in search of work. They have been described as marching along railway tracks "with sacks on their backs and scythes over their shoulders." In the spring, they marched along muddy roads and river banks, heading for the southern regions to be on hand for the plowing. Later, other peasant "armies" marched toward the same areas as reinforcements for the autumn harvest.

There was little order to these seasonal migrations in search of work. A rumor that there was work in a particular province would result in thousands of peasants dashing there. Stepniak observed that in these wanderings "there is neither system nor order. . . . The peasants of the Province of Viatka rush to Samara, whilst those of Samara try their luck in Viatka, and both Samara and Viatka send batches of their men to the Black Sea steppes . . ."

Many of them, of course, never did find work and returned home as destitute as when they had left. Others who did find work often labored as much as sixteen hours a day, slept in the open fields, and survived on near-starvation rations. They returned to their native villages with little or nothing to show for their work.

Besides the seasonal migratory peasant groups, there were individual peasants who resorted to permanent flight from their masters. There are no reliable estimates on the number of individuals over the centuries who ran away from their masters. However, the number was great. For, in addition to runaway individuals, large groups—sometimes a village or several villages— would migrate to what they hoped would be a better place to live. Between 1826 and 1854 alone, 228 separate military detachments were dispatched by the government to restore order in the villages and to round up runaway peasants.

In some instances, a peasant took as much of his master's goods as he possibly could when he fled. His destination was usually the "wild" areas of the empire. There he would join a robber band and prey upon passing travelers or raid outpost settlements. In other cases, the fleeing peasants would voluntarily become servants of new masters who promised to feed them. If caught, a peasant was flogged and returned to his former master or he was exiled to Siberia, sometimes to hard labor in the mines of the area. Neither innumerable government decrees dealing with runaway peasants nor harsh punishments deterred the peasants or those who sheltered them. The flights continued, and in times of droughts, plagues, or political disturbances the number of runaway peasants increased tremendously.

The peasant did not seem to be too fearful of migrating even to distant areas as long as he believed he could find a better livelihood. Stepniak observed that "our peasants have no difficulty whatever in migrating to new places, provided they may start there on the same work and in the same mode of life which has proved itself congenial to them in their old homes. It may be said, without exaggeration, that most of the peasants in the thickly populated central provinces of Russia are permanently on the look-out for some new settlement."

From the time of Ivan the Terrible, Siberia was the favored area for migration, although other areas such as Turkestan were favored, too. At certain times during Ivan's reign, entire areas were depopulated by the migration of peasants. For example, in the 1580s, in the northwest, out of 34,000 settlements listed in the land registers, 83 percent were described as empty. In the region around Pskov, over 85 percent of the homesteads on the rolls were vacant. And in one area of Novgorod, 97 percent of the settlements were unoccupied.

As the government tightened its policy on migration, this condition did not occur so dramatically. Still, the migration went on, with the government preventing it on the one hand and encouraging it on the other. The government tried to enforce the ban on runaways in order to protect the masters, the serf system, its tax rolls, and its recruitment base. On the other hand, it wished to settle the vast areas of Siberia for both economic and political reasons.

Jules Legras, a Frenchman who accompanied the French writer Theophile Gautier on his trip to Russia in 1904, estimated that with the extension of the railroad system to Siberia, there was an annual exodus from European Russia to Siberia of 200,000 to 300,000 peasants. In fact, the population of Siberia between 1897 and 1914 increased from 13 million to 21 million, an increase much greater than that in European Russia.

The number of peasants sentenced to exile in Siberia for various crimes was significant but small compared to the number of those who migrated on their own. The plight of the prisoners, however, was extremely harsh, especially on the trip to their place of exile. The trip was incredibly difficult and was made on foot. The ratio of prisoners who died on the way to Siberia has been estimated as high as 75 percent. Those who had been sentenced to hard labor were sent to extremely isolated areas or to the mines. The other prisoners were given land by the government, and they became state peasants. They were free to come and go but only within their own area. For the first three years of exile, they were exempt from taxes. They were given a horse, a plow, and a few tools. For the first year, they received the same rations as a regular soldier plus two kopecks a day. The wife and each child received half rations and one kopeck a day. In the second year, the subsidy was reduced, and in the third year it ceased. From then on, the exile was completely on his own to face the wilderness and the winter cold with temperatures in some areas as low as 20 to 30 degrees below zero.

13 The Peasant in the City

ALTHOUGH there had always been some movement of peasants from village to city, the tempo of movement began to increase in the early eighteenth century as the problem of finding workers for city factories became increasingly acute. As a result, there was a compulsory assignment of large numbers of peasants to permanent factory work so that industrial enterprises could be maintained. As industrialization increased in the nineteenth century, this movement of peasants was accelerated.

The factory labor force in the cities consisted basically of three kinds of workers: assigned state peasants, serfs who were rented to factory owners by their masters, and hired workers. The first group, composed of serfs who were compelled to work in government-owned factories, was quite large, accounting for almost 32 percent of the total factory labor in 1825. In some factories, they worked only part time, with the rest of the time spent in their agricultural pursuits.

The lords who did not own factories rented their serfs to manufacturers, often herding them together like cattle and driving them to the factories. The efficiency of the peasant worker was low and the morale even lower. One report in the 1840s stated:

> The worst kind of workers are the peasants who are rented out by seigniors to the factories and plants of others. . . . It is useless to expect any diligence or order from them; the factory owner is menaced at every instant by workers running away, cheating, playing knavish tricks. We have heard of these workers, upon whom neither warnings nor threats have any effect, often fleeing the plant in a body, abandoning their work at the most costly moment.

The third group—the hired workers—was composed originally of a variety of persons living in the city, runaway serfs, and persons not attached to any particular class.

As the need for factory labor increased, serfs received permission from their lords, and state peasants received permission from government officials, to leave their villages for work in the city. This meant, in effect, that the peasant was legally free to live and work in the city as a worker but that he remained a serf, subject to traditional duties to his master and subject, too, to being recalled to the village at any time by his master or his mir. It also meant that the peasant as a factory worker belonged, in a sense, to two work groups, the peasantry and the working class, but to only one social group—the peasantry.

The peasant as worker-in-the city was placed in an almost impossible situation. He maintained legal relationships and strong economic and personal ties with his village, yet he was working and living as a member of the industrial proletariat. Many writers in their descriptions of Russian industrial life have stressed the hatred that the peasants, as a result, felt toward factory work. D. Mackenzie Wallace, after noting that this condition made them a class of hybrids—"half-peasants, half-artisans"—observed that "during his residence in the town, his wife and family remained at home, and thither he himself sooner or later returned. . . . The unnatural separation of the artisan from his wife and family leads to very undesirable results." This dislocation affected a considerable number of peasants. It was estimated that in 1897 more than five million villagers were to be found in the cities of European Russia.

Working conditions in these factories were intolerable. Peasant workers were forced to accept all kinds of deductions from their wages—if they received money wages at all—were forced to patronize the company store for their provisions, and were required to work extremely long hours. It was not unusual for children, as well as men, to work twelve, fourteen, even seventeen hours a day. Sometimes, in addition to their work in the factory, they had to do work at home. Some factory owners, in order to keep their own serfs in their factories, substituted hired serfs to fill the quotas for military service demanded by the government.

The physical appearance of the urban peasant worker was described by George M. Dallas, who was United States Minister to Russia in the late 1830s:

> The streets afford at every step something for comment. Here, for instance, comes a mere laborer. His covering is a sheepskin cloak, the wool inwards, lapping over in front, and kept together by a coarse and often colored girdle. It is dirty externally beyond conception, smeared black with grease and smells most offensively. He wears a hat of no shape, with the band drawn tight halfway in the crown. His feet are hid in a sort of matting, composed of strips about an inch wide and plaited in the form of a moccasin. His beard hangs a foot from his chin. His moustache is thick and conceals both lips, and his hair, coarse and matted, is cut close and round, just along the rim of his hat. His neck is entirely bare, and his skin is everywhere pallid, dark, and dusty. This is an exact delineation of the mass of serfs or peasants whom you meet by thousands at work along the wharves, or on the public buildings, or at the highways.

The day-to-day existence of the peasant worker was described by an English visitor to Russia just before the emancipation of the serfs in 1861. The following is an account of an interview he had with a peasant who worked in a cotton mill:

> I earn four rubles [about two dollars] a month [the peasant said]. My time is all spent in the mill—from five o'clock in the morning until eight o'clock at night. My wife and two daughters work on the fields belonging to the baron five days every week in summer. They get no

wages. In winter they do any kind of work required of them by the steward.

My son, who is seventeen years old, works also in the mill, and gets two rubles a month. We have three *dessiatines* [2.7 acres per *dessiatine*] of land. It is our own; so is the house. We can only raise a few potatoes, cabbages, and carrots. The women do this work. We keep a pig, and we have some ducks. We eat them. We get black bread from the *econom* [the steward's shop]. This is deducted from our wages. We pay no obrok from these wages, no taxes. Our work is counted for this; the steward manages all that.

Somehow I am always in debt to the steward's office. I have worked ten years in the mill and am a good spinner. I don't know what we shall do when we get our freedom. We shall not work any more, I suppose. I may go begging; it is an easy life. I am now unfit for outdoor work; but my son is able; let him cultivate the land. We are three thousand souls on this estate. A thousand nearly are away and pay forty rubles obrok each a year. They pay their own passports and taxes besides.

As industrialization increased and became more sophisticated, the use of reluctant and inefficient serfs proved unprofitable. By the end of the nineteenth century, a free-labor system became widespread. The effect of this emerging working class had a direct bearing on events leading up to the Revolution of 1917—and after.

14 Emancipation

THE entire system of serf labor in the factories was archaic. As Russia slowly began to industrialize, it became apparent that it was necessary to substitute a system of free factory labor for the patchwork system that existed. Serfdom was hurting not only manufacturing but agriculture, which had barely changed in hundreds of years. And agriculture was still the occupation for an overwhelming section of the population. In 1860, for instance, less than 8 percent of the population of seventy-four million lived in cities. Fewer than one million persons worked in factories; the rest made their living primarily from the land.

Most important, perhaps, was the fact that the peasants themselves were becoming more and more restive and, in some cases, violent and rebellious. Other groups in Russia, such as the intellectuals, were also beginning not only to sympathize with the plight of the peasants but to work actively on their behalf.

The intellectuals, although numerically a small group, almost unanimously supported emancipation. In spite of official censorship, antiserfdom ideas made their way into newspaper articles, magazines, and books. Outright opposition to serfdom was spread by means of handbills and manuscripts that were passed from hand to hand to avoid the censorship.

Actually, emancipation had been under discussion for almost a century by one or another of Russia's rulers. Catherine the Great, who never had the slightest intention of acting on emancipation and who was the source of some of the most vicious antipeasant decrees, nevertheless paid emancipation lip service. Paul I showed no interest in the question, although he took a few ameliorating measures on behalf of the peasants. Alexander I, a professed liberal like his grandmother Catherine, also gave the matter lip service but no action.

Nicholas I, who has been described as strong in force of mind and firm in resolve, gave the question serious attention and considered various compromises between the landowners and the peasants. He was haunted by the Pugachev Rebellion and subsequent peasant outbreaks. On a report from one of his ministers in which the word "progress" was used, he wrote over it: "Progress? What progress? This word must be deleted from official terminology!" Nevertheless, he said to his Council of State in 1842:

"There is no question that serfdom, as it now exists among us, is an evil, palpable and evident to everyone, but to touch it now would be even more disastrous. The late Emperor Alexander, at the beginning of his reign, had intentions to give freedom to the serfs, but later he gave up this idea entirely as premature and impossible of execution. I, too, will never do it, reckoning that if the time when it will be possible to take this measure is still far distant, then all talk about it at present is nothing other than a criminal attempt upon the general peace and on the welfare of the state. The Pugachev rising shows how far peasant violence is able to go. . . . But if the present situation is such that it cannot continue, and if at the same time, decisive measures to end it are not possible without general commotion, then it is necessary at least to prepare the way for a gradual transition to another order of things, and without being afraid of change, calmly consider its usefulness and its consequences. It is not necessary to give freedom, but it is necessary to work out a way to a transitional stage. . . ."

Fourteen years later, in 1856, a few days after the end of the Crimean War, Czar Alexander II made the following pronouncement before an assembly of nobles in Moscow:

"Certainly, as you yourselves know, the existing manner of possessing serfs cannot remain unchanged. It is better to abolish serfdom from above than to await the time when it will begin to abolish itself from below."

Although the czar was perturbed by the possibly dangerous results of continuing the system of serfdom, the nobles were not. For a while, nothing was done, and it was assumed that, as had happened so many times before, positive action would not be taken. But the nobles were wrong. Subsequently, Alexander appointed a Chief Committee for Peasant Affairs, under the leadership of his brother, Grand Duke Constantine, to examine the question. Again little was accomplished, but at the end of 1857, when, in a series of decrees, Alexander supported emancipation of the Lithuanian peasants, the proverbial die was cast. At long last, action was being taken on the question of emancipation of the serfs.

Many landowners resisted bitterly and argued violently against emancipation. Other landowners, however, did support freedom for the serfs, some out of humanitarian reasons and others out of loyalty to the wishes of the czar. Every section of the population and people in all kinds of work and professions expressed themselves on this most volatile social and economic problem of the time.

The writers, freed at last from official censorship now that the czar himself was in favor of emancipation, poured out numerous articles on how the peasants had been wronged and how giving them their freedom would open up a bright new world for oppressed and oppressor alike. Their articles were filled with the words "humanity," "brotherhood," "equality," and "love." As one writer phrased it, they "displayed a feverish excitement which demanded a liberal use of superlatives."

The reformers and abolitionists, who had been preaching against serfdom in low voices and in fear of arrest, now stridently spoke of the end of "slavery," "inequality," and "man's inhumanity to man." They predicted that at long last the promised land was possible where all men would be brothers and a high morality would prevail.

Lawyers presented long arguments that the landowners never had a legal right to the land in the first place. Historians noted that since ownership of peasants had been given to the nobles for services and obligations that were no longer required of them, there was no historical reason for prolonging serfdom. Economists and political scientists observed that if Russia was to become a truly modern industrial nation, it had to do away with its feudal system of labor and introduce free labor in the same manner as had advanced industrialized countries. The educated youth of the country ardently championed emancipation and joyously proclaimed that Russia was at long last discarding this badge of national shame and dishonor. Older men joined them—even those who owned serfs—and spoke of the new humanitarianism. Even some army officials, some of whom were landowners themselves, supported emancipation, claiming that if Russia was to have a modern army with trained reserves, it could be accomplished only if there was an end to serfdom.

The opponents of emancipation were just as vocal and just as convinced that freeing the serfs would destroy the character and structure of the country and plunge both peasant and lord into an economic, political, and social maelstrom. Almost all of the opposition came from the nobles, and they found few allies among other sections of the population.

Basically, their arguments were the same as those they had been propounding for decades. The comment in the 1840s by Count Nesselrode, the Minister of Foreign Affairs, was typical of those in the 1860s: "All the plans of emancipation . . . can only lead to peasant riots and the ruin of the nobility."

Some landowners claimed that they would be ruined economically if the serfs were taken away from them since they had no other source of revenue except income from the estates upon which the serfs worked. Their profits were too small, they argued, and it would bankrupt them to have to pay wages for work previously done for nothing.

Still others claimed that to abolish serfdom would bring disaster to the state inasmuch as the compensation that the landowners would demand would bring financial ruin to government, destruction of the nobility as a class, and the loss of autocratic power by the czar. Some feared the prophecy of the radicals, who theorized that an increased working class would eventually become a revolutionary threat to the existing system.

The argument that the serf was too ignorant and backward to conduct his own affairs was raised over and over again. It was endlessly pointed out that if the peasant was lazy, irresponsible, and even rebellious under the stern hand of his master, he would be much more so without his master's guidance. They echoed the arguments of the historian Nicholas Karamzin, who some years previously had written that without the tutelage of their educated masters, the ignorant peasants would become idlers, drunkards, and criminals. "Serfs can be liberated as soon as it is possible for wolves to be fully fed while sheep remain uninjured," he wrote.

Despite all these objections, the nobles limited their opposition to verbal complaints and eventually ceased even verbal opposition. They finally took the position that even though they disagreed they would not openly disobey their czar. Reluctantly, they finally took part in the selection of provincial committees in the various sections of the empire that were to present proposals on matters such as the size of the peasant allotments and redemption payments for the landowners. Editing commissions were set up to turn out the details of the emancipation law.

On March 3, 1861 (February 19, old calendar), Alexander signed the emancipation decree, which was read in the senate on March 14 and published on March 17. On the following Sunday in all the churches of the country, the decree was read aloud by the priests. In some areas, the announcement was greeted with cheers, in others with sullen disapproval, and in still others with indifference. Prince Kropotkin reported some years later that there was jubilation in St. Petersburg, with crowds outside the Winter Palace cheering the czar. On the other hand, the American Minister to

Russia reported that he drove through the capital on the Sunday the emancipation was read in the churches and that emancipation "was received tranquilly and there was no appearance of excitement anywhere. I met the emperor several times, but his passage through the streets seemed to create no special enthusiasm."

The emancipation law, which was greeted with such mixed feelings, had three main points. The first was that the serfs immediately would have the same rights as free rural persons and that the authority of the serfowner would be replaced by communal self-government. The second was that the communes would, if possible, retain the land they actually held, and, in return, would pay the landowner a certain amount of yearly dues in the form of money or labor. The third was that the government would give credit to communes to purchase the lands ceded to them. Domestic serfs were tied to their masters for two more years, after which they were free but had no claim to a share of land.

Altogether, approximately 23 million serfs received their freedom from about 104,000 landowners on whose estates they lived.

15 Post-Emancipation

EMANCIPATION was hailed at the time it was proclaimed as the act that would usher in a great new era for Russia. Some persons believed that the empire would now take its place among the more advanced nations of the world. Among the major nations of the Western world, only the United States was more backward in this regard. It still had slavery, which was not abolished until two years after Russia freed the serfs.

The czar's decree had brought to an end hundreds of years of enslavement. At the same time, it did away with a social order that legalized the superiority of one class over another. In practice, however, it all didn't work out so well. Full civil rights were not granted the freed peasants. They still had some restrictions on their freedom of movement. And in many cases they did not become the owners of the land they tilled.

While many nonpeasant, antiserfdom forces hailed emancipation when it was proclaimed, most of the peasants greeted the new law with sullen resentment. They had no understanding of the full text of the document, which ran for nearly four hundred printed pages, was divided into seventeen separate statutes and two appendices, and was full of difficult language. One historian noted: "These laws of 1861 were so verbose, so full of variables, so loaded down with qualifications and exceptions, and in general so astonishingly involved and complicated, that it is difficult to understand how any serf could ever by any possibility have known what rights might be hidden in this legislative haystack." In 1906, more than forty years after the law was passed, the Ministry of the Interior reported that the peasant land laws were "incomplete, inexact, and in some instances even contradictory."

However, it was not the difficult language that disturbed the peasant—he would never read the full text, anyway—but the substance of the act as it affected his day-to-day existence. Would it better his standard of living? Would it give him good land and enough of it to feed his family properly? And, finally, would he have to buy the land that he felt, historically, belonged to him? For as he had always phrased it, "We are yours, but the land is ours."

It was for these reasons that even on the day the substance of the act was read to him in the church he had listened with sullen anger. Nowhere in the act did he hear the various answers to his questions. In fact, the confused language convinced him that this was not the true act at all. He believed that the czar would issue the real emancipation decree shortly, and this one would give him all the things he wanted.

"To their candid, unsophisticated minds," wrote Stepniak, "it seemed utterly incredible that their czar should have wronged them so bitterly as to the land. They obstinately repeated that their freedom, that is, the Emancipation Act, had been tampered with by the nobility, who had concealed the czar's real freedom, which had been quite a different thing. The most emphatic declarations made before the peasants' deputies and elders by the emperor's ministers and by the emperor in person could not disabuse them. They persisted in believing against belief."

The noble had quite the opposite reaction from that of the peasant. He had feared emancipation would ruin him; instead, in many cases, it saved him. A number of serf owners had become impoverished, and now they had access to cash. And the noble had no obligation to the peasant. As far as he was concerned, the peasant was now free to starve. And if he wished to work, the noble might hire him, at the noble's terms, to work on his estate. One such postemancipation agreement between freed serf and former master read: "I, the undersigned, agree to submit myself to all the rules and customs in force on the estate of *N. N.* During the period of work, I will be perfectly obedient to *N. N.*'s managers, and will not refuse to work at night, not only such work as I have undertaken to do, as set forth above, but any other work that may be required of me. Moreover, I have no right to keep Sundays and holidays."

All was not well, however, for the former serf owner. The peasants often refused to work for their former masters, even if they were in need of employment. D. Mackenzie Wallace related the reaction of a steward when peasants refused to work on their former master's estate: "The peasants have not been improved by liberty," the steward said. "They now work less and drink more than they did in the times of serfage, and if you say a word to them they'll go away, and not work for you at all."

Still, the noble had been—and still was—the bulwark of czardom. The government tried to help him with such measures as the establishment of the Nobles' Land Bank, from which he could borrow money at easy terms.

For the peasant, there were few positive actions taken to alleviate his dissatisfaction with emancipation. One of these was the appointment of Arbiters of the Peace, local proprietors in each district. Their task was to regulate relations between the freed peasant and the landowner, explain the law to the former serfs, and help them with their self-government. Despite this effort, disturbances were reported in almost all the provinces during the first five months of 1861—of which 718 required armed intervention by government troops. Stepniak noted that they finally subsided only after "ten years of incessant persuasion through the medium of speeches, ukazes, flogging, and an occasional shooting." As one peasant himself phrased it: "There is no order now; the people have been spoiled; it was better in the time of the masters."

Actually, life for the peasants had changed little for the better, if at all. They were still hungry. They still had their debts. In some cases, their debts were even higher than before because of excessive prices that were charged for redeeming the land.

The peasant's disillusion was deep because his expectations had been high. Intellectuals and reformers could find comfort in the fact that emancipation had been won and that a new social order was possible for Russia. The peasant knew only that his manner of living had not improved. In fact, he now found that money obligations were more difficult to pay off than work obligations. He no longer had the small protection of the master when, in some cases, he could graze his cattle on the master's land, come to him for help in bad times, and receive firewood and logs to build his hut. All was now a money relationship, and he simply didn't have any. Still, the master could no longer flog him or have jurisdiction over him. Thus, as one peasant said upon being asked his reaction to emancipation: "How shall I say to you? It is both better and worse!"

Because of the peasant's inability to pay the large sums needed for redemption of the land, over a large part of Russia ownership passed into the hands of the village community or mir. In many cases, the mir apportioned the land on the old basis of the peasant family or household. The landowning nobility retained about 45 percent of the best land. And the townspeople—merchants and honorary citizens—bought up a great deal of land from the nobles, reducing the amount of good land available to the peasants. The ideal of some that the peasant would become an independent farmer was not realized. The mir, in effect, took the place of the landowner. And in the mir, the more aggressive peasants ruled over the others. With the absence of the power of the former masters, the government now exercised more direct jurisdiction over the peasants.

New governmental administrative units were set up to aid the government in its now-expanded role of supervising the peasants. One such unit was the *volost,* which was a form of township composed of a number of adjoining communes. It had its own officials and its own assembly, which were selected from the member communes. Its courts were composed of judges elected by the assembly. The volost had many features of self-government and fairly broad powers over its members.

In the years following emancipation, it became obvious that what was developing was an impoverished free peasantry in thousands of communes that were serving as regulatory bodies, in effect, for the state. Many peasants defaulted on their obligations and drifted to the cities or became seasonal workers in lumbering, coal mining, and other fields. They were joined by the former household serfs who were landless and became the recruits for the new industrial army that was filling the factories—and the slums—of the cities. They supplied the brawn for the growing industrialization pursued by the government toward the close of the nineteenth century. At the same time, the peasants on the land were heavily taxed to help finance the empire's frantic dash to become an industrialized country. As a result, poverty in the villages became more acute, and poor working conditions in the city gave rise to an embittered working class.

Socially, the peasants were as isolated from the mainstream of Russian life as they had been before emancipation. The peasant family lost much of its cohesiveness and, in a sense, its strength. Sons and brothers drifted off to the cities to join the growing working class, hoping to escape from the wretched poverty of the village. They no longer had their ties with their village, legally enforceable before emancipation.

Culturally, the Russian peasant did not participate in the rapid progress being made by many Russians of the middle and upper classes. Educationally, he was as poorly off as he was before emancipation. As one authority, N. N. Kovalevsky, noted: "The principal objective of the government was not to spread popular education as widely and as rapidly as possible. It was to ward off some kind of danger to the nation because the people will acquire too much knowledge unnecessarily through schools and books, and will not broaden their intellectual horizon. There are still not a few persons who are convinced that popular ignorance is the best guarantee of social order."

Sadly—and significantly for the future history of Russia—emancipation did not solve the problems of the peasantry. The results were a far cry from the hopes that emancipation had raised not only in Russia but as far away as the United States. For example, the *New York Times,* in March 1865, had commented: "Russia is on a sure, steady career of progress and reform. With the new provincial bodies, and the spread of common schools and newspapers (of which we hear such encouraging accounts), she will soon educate a mass of intelligent and orderly citizens who will be fully capable of governing themselves."

16 The New Politics and the Peasant

As Russia moved toward the twentieth century, it was a country out of joint. A large number of its educated citizens were out of sympathy with the nation's rulers, practices, and ideas. The educated youth were hostile to the nation's traditions. The rising industrial class demanded more profits but alienated its employees by offering them starvation wages and miserable working conditions. The small middle class was smug in its material comforts and disdainful of the coarseness and ignorance of the peasants and city workers. The nobles refused to relinquish their special privileges and pretended that the ills of the nation were the fault of lazy peasants, militant workers, and fuzzy-minded intellectuals. The government acted, in essence, as if its power were God-given, and grudgingly made concessions on the one hand while it held the whip—and used it—with the other.

In the past, groups composed primarily of students and intellectuals had sympathized with the plight of the peasants, mainly out of humanitarian feelings. Now, however, they were drawn to the peasantry by an almost religious mystique. Others went to them with social or political programs that they believed would once and for all rid Russia of poverty and tyranny and make it a land of plenty and brotherhood.

They saw in the simple, primitive peasant the answer to the depravity and selfishness of Russian society, guided by a ruthless autocrat, useless nobles, materialistic merchants, and rapacious capitalists. As a counterforce to these elements, they elevated the peasant into something almost holy, someone who could give Russia inspiration for a good and decent life. Personally, the students and intellectuals hoped to find by contact with the earthy peasant a cure for their own world-weariness, frustration, and disgust with the materialistic world that seemed to offer no hope, joy, or love.

They viewed official Russia as a cesspool that needed a thorough cleaning so that the people could once again become honest, upright human beings. They fulminated against the evils of Russian society, especially against the poverty and degradation of the peasantry.

Persons in many walks of life began to examine not only society but themselves. They questioned their thoughts, attitudes, actions, goals, even the way they dressed and wore their hair. Everything about the established order of things appeared to them evil and degraded, and they wanted to have little or nothing to do with the so-called establishment.

"All Russia cursed the past and leaned out toward the future," the writer Tikhomirov observed. "All men began reasoning, criticizing, denying, inquiring.

"The fathers—the older generation of Russia—were frightfully corrupted by the reign of Nicholas; they felt themselves guilty toward Russia, toward their children, toward their conscience. How had they been able to bear the despotism of Nicholas? How had they been able to suffer . . . and to participate in all the frightful abuses of serfdom? How had they allowed science to be persecuted for thirty-five years? Whither had all this led Russia? The fathers felt guilt. They would have liked to have made themselves scarce, to have sunk under the earth. The children—the younger generation—could cry out with perfect freedom, with all the force of a really honest indignation, of young enthusiasm, and of inexperience.

"Then certain sides of Russian general philosophy, certain characteristic traits of the intelligentsia, manifested themselves in the most ridiculous and most exaggerated fashion. The tendency toward democratic ideas manifested itself occasionally by the most exaggerated aversion from everything that was aristocratic, from everything that smacked of the nobility, and consequently from all the formalities of superficial civilization. Unclean faces, disheveled hair, dirty and fantastic clothes were to be seen. In conversation, to give proof of a willful coarseness, the language of peasants was used. There was contempt for the hypocritical and conventional formal morality. There was contempt for the ridiculous traditions which had so long been considered the expression of wisdom of the State. There was indignation at the oppression borne by the individual. All this was expressed by an absolute negation of authority of all kinds, and in the most exaggerated tendency toward liberty."

It was in this situation that the reformers and revolutionaries carried on their activities. Among those persons who went to the peasantry, the most active during the two decades after emancipation were the Narodniki, or Populists. Their following comprised a varied assortment of persons from many walks of life—students, intellectuals, and liberals. Their movement was loosely organized and included persons who were determined to "go to the people" as social workers, manual laborers, doctors and nurses, or revolutionary agitators. Most of them were antigovernment and, as they phrased it, "for the people." Many of them considered the peasantry as embodying the best virtues and as being the basic force for any significant or revolutionary change in the country. The political activists among them believed that agitation for land reforms arising out of agrarian unrest was the way to generate revolutionary momentum.

The Populists were convinced that the village communes as an indigenous structure had the necessary elements to become the basis for a Russian socialism. They saw the village commune as a model for free productive associations similar to those advocated by the then popular French utopian socialists. They hoped that, by peacefully converting the village communes to a socialist form, Russia could avoid the industrial capitalism that existed in many parts of Western Europe.

The Populists viewed the commune as "an expression of natural equality, togetherness, unselfishness, and cooperativeness." They ignored the fact that the communes were also dominated by the heads of households or the kulaks, and that, to a large extent, they were land-distributing and regulating bodies performing a variety of administrative work for the government. Critics of the Populists claimed that they idealized the peasants and their communes and overlooked the evils. They compared this to the idealization of the "noble savage," which had been in vogue in other countries.

Through visits to the peasants, working with them, and especially through the written word, their propaganda flooded the villages. In one summer alone, in 1874, thousands of Populist students invaded the countryside to fraternize with and "educate" the peasants. On this occasion as on so many others, they were greeted with some curiosity but mostly with suspicion and hostility. In a few instances, the peasants even betrayed them to the police. The aloofness of the peasants—even their betrayal of their self-proclaimed benefactors—did not dissuade the Populists from their endeavors to save them. A typical Populist appeal to the peasants was the following:

> Though they work a hundred times more than the landlord, the peasants are incomparably poorer than he is.
>
> The time has come to escape from poverty and darkness.
>
> We, your brothers, we turn to you, the oppressed, and we call on you in the name of eternal justice.
>
> Rise up against this regime of injustice, which is unworthy of man and unworthy of the highest moral consciousness of the land. Rise, brothers.
>
> We demand the abolition of all dues. This land which we are compelled to redeem has been ours throughout the centuries. On it lived our fathers, our grandfathers, and our ancestors. When we were slaves

of the noble landlords we farmed this land. The nobles no longer exist. What does this mean? Merely that we have separated from them. Our land has returned to us. Why on earth must we pay for it?

Further, we demand a general redistribution of the land, both that which belongs to the peasants as well as that which is owned by the state and the nobles. It must be redistributed among ourselves according to justice, so that each has what he needs.

The Populists, disguised as beggars, peddlers, or tramps, walked over a good part of Russia preaching their message to the peasants. Sometimes, they established themselves in villages as tailors, healers, or menders. They made friends with the local innkeepers in order to be close to the center of peasant gatherings. They went out of their way to enlist the village teachers in their groups. They gave away newspapers and booklets to the youth and any others who could read. In their literature, they hammered away at the idea that the peasant would never be free until he recovered for himself the goods that the masters unjustly kept for themselves.

Among the various Populist groups was the Zemlya i Volya (Land and Liberty) movement, which arose in the 1870s. Its members have been described as "rebels who idealized the people." They hoped that when freedom had been achieved there would appear political forms based on the communes and on some kind of federation. They did not predict the precise form of government that would arise and left this matter "to the effective will of the nation." Their belief was partially stated in this excerpt from one of their pamphlets: "Society must understand that it must not get down on its knees and whine for liberty, but conquer it. It must understand this and organize itself for the fight against the government."

Basically an agrarian socialist movement, the Land and Liberty group lasted for only a few years. Some of its members then joined other agrarian reform groups or terrorist organizations.

A more radical group, the Narodnaya Volya (The Will of the People) arose in 1879 after splitting with the Zemlya i Volya. It engaged in various forms of terrorism, including the assassination of government leaders. Its members believed that by this method the government would fall and the peasant would be free. One of the victims was Czar Alexander II, who was assassinated in 1881. A member of The Will of the People, condemned to death with several others because of his terrorist activities, wrote:

"We have no regrets at having to die. We die for an idea. And if we do have any regret it is only that the significance of our deaths lies merely in the shame it puts on the dying monarchy and not something better, and that before our death we have not done what we wanted to do."

Eventually, some members of this group joined the Social Democrats and later became members of the Bolshevik party. The majority of them, however, combined with other Populist groups in 1902 to form the Socialist Revolutionaries.

The turning away from Populism by many of the Narodniki was based, in part, on the peasant rejection of their doctrine of agrarian socialism. The peasants simply were not interested in socialism. After numerous rebuffs, a number of Populists lost faith in the peasants as a revolutionary force and in terrorism as a means of overthrowing the government. Instead, they embraced the Marxist concept that stressed the revolutionary potential of the working class instead of the peasantry. They supported Marxist leaders such as Lenin, who hurled one polemic after another at the Populists. He and others insisted that even though the peasants formed 90 percent of the population, it was the industrial worker who would be the bulwark of the revolution.

The Marxists rejected the concept of the commune as a base for socialism and the desire of the Populists to prevent the rise of Russian capitalism. They saw capitalism as an advance over the existing agrarian society. In effect, they wanted capitalism to become more firmly established so that they could then, through an enlarged working class, abolish both capitalism and czarism and in their place establish socialism.

17 The Years Before the 1917 Revolution

FOR rural Russia, the several decades preceding the Russian Revolution of 1917 were years of recurring agrarian crises. The unresolved peasant question continually plagued the government, forcing it to take certain measures to increase production, stem peasant dissatisfaction, and blunt agitational political opposition.

Even though there were signs here and there that a few technological changes were being put into effect, especially on large estates, the general appearance of the Russian countryside and its people had changed very little. It was what the American historian G. T. Robinson referred to as the "mature and complex primitiveness of Russian peasant agriculture." Robinson remarked, too, that "it was not the primitiveness of pioneering, not new and raw, but stained and weathered, and worn round by time: not the beginning of a new history so much as some late chapter of an old one. All about, in the compact village, in the intricate pattern of the fields, in the routine of the seeding and the harvest, there were the evidences of a venerable tradition."

However, other things were changing that affected agricultural production: the fluctuation of grain prices, the changing emphasis from subsistence production to production for the marketplace, the new tax structure that had been occasioned by emancipation, and the new relationship of the peasant to the land. The peasant was now being forced to raise crops not for his own use but for cash in a marketplace in which prices fluctuated. His taxes were in cash, not labor or kind, and they had become even more burdensome with the post-emancipation redemption dues he now had to pay for gaining possession of the land. This resulted in greater debts, further inability to pay taxes and redemption dues, and progressively decreasing land allotments.

The average land allotment in European Russia decreased from 5.1 dessiatines per male peasant in 1860 to 2.7 dessiatines in 1900, a decrease of 47 percent. With half as much land with which to gain a livelihood, it was little wonder that agricultural production dropped and that the peasant was in dire trouble.

For those peasants who supplemented their income by working for others, the wages were unbelievably low. The average wage for an agricultural laborer was one ruble and eight kopecks a day, or about 54 cents—without rations. This was at the height of the agricultural season; those who worked on a year-round basis were paid much less. Except for black bread, which was very cheap, most other items were relatively expensive. For instance, in 1913 sugar cost sixteen kopecks a pound, or about one-seventh of a day's wage. A pair of workman's boots cost about six rubles, or about five days' wages.

The manner of obtaining work for itinerant agricultural laborers was satisfactory in those areas where the zemstvos provided them with shelter, meals, and medical attention. However, in other areas there were no such accommodations, and the workers "were soaked by the rain, shivered, starved, sickened, and died," as others had done for many years before them.

Those agricultural workers who tried to better their conditions by organizing work protests or strikes did so at great peril to themselves. If a worker quit before his contract expired, he could be imprisoned for a month. If a group of workers quit or forced others to do so, they could be imprisoned for up to a year. Members of an organization who coerced or incited agricultural laborers to stop work in violation of a contract could be imprisoned for up to four years.

In 1891, a famine struck the peasantry with disaster force. When it came, the peasant had been so beaten by exorbitant taxes that he had no surplus whatsoever to guard him against crop failure. For under the intense capital industry development program of Finance Minister Sergei Witte, the peasantry had been forced to pay, through taxes, a large share of the cost.

While the peasants were grumbling over their troubles, the workers in the city were becoming more and more restive over their poor conditions. The government was torn not only by severe economic problems but by strikes of workers and demands by liberal and radical elements for widespread political reforms. In addition, in 1904 Russia had become embroiled in a war with Japan over power in the Far East. Within eighteen months, Russia had been severely beaten militarily and had suffered the shame of defeat by a hitherto supposedly weak country. All these events contributed to the outbreak of the Revolution of 1905.

During these times, various political parties formulated agrarian programs, hoping to enlist the peasantry under their particular banners.

In June 1905, the Socialist Revolutionaries, who had a strong base among the peasants, held a conference at which it was concluded that the time had finally come to put an end to the old order. They declared that the land "ought to belong to the whole people, and be employed equally, but only by those who themselves work upon it, and in such quantity as each himself may cultivate."

The Social Democratic party had, in 1903, split into two groups: a radical group, subsequently known as the Bolsheviks, and a moderate group, subsequently called the Mensheviks. At various conferences in 1905, the Mensheviks came out in support of the peasants, even to their seizure of land. However, they did not seem to have a dynamic program, and they continued to debate the problem. The Bolsheviks called on the peasants for "a collective refusal to pay taxes, or to furnish recruits, or to fulfill the orders and commands of the government and its agents." They supported confiscation of land by the peasants. They viewed the peasantry as an ally of the working class but "elementary and lacking in political consciousness." Actually, they did not expect the peasantry to be of major importance in the overthrow of czarism and the establishment of socialism. Nevertheless, in one of their resolutions, the Bolsheviks noted that "Social Democracy should in every case and under all conditions steadfastly aspire to organize the village proletariat independently, and to explain to them the irreconcilable opposition between their interests and those of the peasant bourgeoisie."

Events at the time gave rise to a meeting of peasant representatives in the All-Russian Peasants' Union, which met near Moscow in the summer of 1905. Sentiment varied from radical to moderate. The program that emerged was one that supported land for the peasants; universal suffrage; the calling of the Duma, the national assembly; and more local autonomy in the hands of locally elected officials. Three months later, in November, during the hectic events of the 1905 revolution, the Peasants' Union met again. As at the previous meeting, there were speeches on the peasant situation that ranged from fiery to moderate. Long debates took place on the problems of land and liberty. One fairly typical expression of opinion was the following:

> Land is not the product of human hands. It was created by the Holy Spirit, and therefore should not be bought and sold. No one really bought it [in the beginning] for money; somebody knew how to take it away from the peasants. . . . Whether the land was taken away in the time of our ancestors by the czars, or by the princes, or by someone else, we do not know, and in any case we are not to blame. Therefore, it is not necessary to pay compensation to anyone.
>
> It is necessary to take the land and give it to the working peasants. Pay compensation! What for?
>
> Comrades! Let us not make the mistake that our fathers made. In 1861 they [the masters] gave us a little in order that the people should

not take everything. The peasants were ignorant and unorganized then, but now things are different. With millions of voices we insistently declare the sacredness of our right to the land. If persuasion does not help, then, friends, plowmen, get up, awake, straighten your backs! For the moment we shall lay our plows aside, and take up the club.

By and large, the Peasants' Union as well as the radical political parties did not have too great an effect on the actions of the peasants themselves, who during this period were expressing their anger by means of violent disturbances. Actually, most of the peasants showed little interest in the wide ramifications of political change. Their primary interest was their unfettered ownership of the land.

The peasant unrest during the Revolution of 1905 followed many of the patterns of previous peasant disturbances—intimidation of landowners, burning of manor houses, cutting of timber, and looting. On occasion, however, their actions had a more direct revolutionary significance. There were a number of cases in which the peasants actually tried to expropriate estate lands and thus directly challenged governmental authority and law. All together, it was estimated that more than two thousand estates were destroyed in 1905.

Most times, the peasants immediately dispersed upon the arrival of military detachments, but there were a number of instances in which they did not and they were fired upon by the troops. Many of the peasants who revolted received severe floggings from the authorities. There were cases, too, in which the troops were ordered to burn down the huts of rebellious peasants. "Take the sternest measures to bring the disorders to an end," ordered Minister of the Interior P. N. Durnovo to a provincial governor. "It is a useful thing to wipe the rebellious village off the face of the earth, and to exterminate the rebels themselves without mercy, by force of arms."

The reaction of the nobility to the events of 1905 was a combination of fear, hostility, and a desire to find some way out of the dangerous situation. They held several conferences in which they insisted that the government take the sternest measures to put down the rebellious peasants and reaffirmed their faith in the supreme autocratic power. The most conservative of the nobles, through such organizations as the anti-Semitic Union of the Russian People, carried out counterattacks on intellectuals, workers, peasants, and especially against Jews in a series of bloody pogroms.

A few nobles, realizing that positive action should be taken to blunt the anger of the peasants, suggested that some land be given to them. For example, D. F. Trepov, the governor general of St. Petersburg, said to Witte, president of the Committee of Ministers, subsequent to the 1905 outbreaks: "I myself am a landed proprietor, and I shall be very glad indeed to surrender without compensation one-half of my land, since I am persuaded that only under this condition shall I succeed in keeping the other half for myself."

The bitterest attack from the nobles was on the entire concept of the village communes. At their conferences, speaker after speaker attacked them saying that "the commune is based upon socialistic foundations" or that "if the state wishes to set a limit to socialism, it ought to abolish the commune." Actually, the nobles had come to the realization that the best way to lessen peasant unrest and tie the peasant closer to the government and the status quo was to make as many peasants as possible full-fledged owners of private property. In this way, they would have property of their very own to defend instead of being allied to their fellow peasants in the commune. If the peasants would defend their own land, they reasoned, the peasants would not attack theirs. In fact, they even hoped that they might be able to depend upon the more prosperous landed peasants to help defend them against attacks from those who were landless.

The events of the Revolution of 1905 convinced the government that it had to make some fundamental changes in the agrarian situation. Mainly through the guidance and efforts of the minister of the interior, F. A. Stolypin, the government issued a number of far-reaching decrees. Almost all of them had the frank purpose of strengthening the landed gentry and creating allies for them among the better-off peasants. These decrees gave the peasant more personal liberty and freed him from the jurisdiction of the commune. They made it easier for him to become an individual landowner by giving him easy credit in the newly established Peasants' Land Bank and canceling his redemption debt.

These acts were designed to break up the mir, in which the government had now lost faith as a conservative social institution. They promoted Stolypin's basic idea of placing "a wager on the strong." In essence, this slogan meant that the government wished to split the peasantry by developing a class of independent, economically strong peasant proprietors that would have a firm attachment to the concept of private property. As property owners, these "strong" peasants would support the estate system and the government against the "weak" or landless peasants.

Stolypin himself spoke out on this subject at a meeting of the Third Duma, which had been convened as a result of the Revolution of 1905. "The government has placed its wager, not on the needy and the drunken, but on the sturdy and the strong— on the sturdy individual proprietor who is called upon to play a part in the reconstruction of our czardom on strong monarchical foundations."

In the decade between the issuing of these decrees and the outbreak of the Revolution of 1917, progress was made in putting them into action. By the eve of the revolution, small farmers owned about two-thirds of all the land in European Russia that was outside the public domain. The commune did, indeed, lose much of its power and influence. Likewise, the old peasant household also lost its power and influence. As a result of government decree, the head of the family was the sole owner of the alloted property and did not have to share it with anyone else in the family. Thus, all other members of the family lost their property rights and became landless. By breaking the collective aspect of the commune and the household, the government made strides in promoting individualism among the peasantry.

The period between the revolutions of 1905 and 1917 was one of great change for the peasant. His relationships changed with his household, his commune, and his fellow peasants. The strip that characterized each household's plowable land in the holding of the commune changed to plots of land owned individually. Peasants joined cooperative societies to promote the production and marketing of goods. Many peasants felt freer to move eastward, and from 1906 to 1915 almost 3.5 million peasants settled in Siberia.

Whether all these changes benefited the peasants as a group is debatable. The unrestricted sale of land allowed rich peasants to buy more land, especially from their poverty-stricken brothers who then joined the rural or urban proletariat. The peasant community was split even more than it had been between the haves and the have-nots. Stolypin's "wager on the strong" had indeed helped to make part of the peasantry well-off, independent rural property owners. However, it also helped to turn another part into permanently landless rural wage earners or into urban workers. As the Revolution of 1917 dramatically pointed out, Stolypin lost his wager, except that his "sturdy and strong" peasants—the kulaks—proved their stubbornness and strength some years later in their opposition to the agricultural policies of the Communists.

18 Revolution, Civil War, and Reconstruction

IN March 1917, the czar and his government were overthrown. By then, 12 million Russians had been mobilized to fight on the side of the Allies in World War I. The toll of Russians killed in the war was almost 2 million, of which the overwhelmingly majority were peasants. The peasants had been recruited from all parts of Russia. In most cases, they were ill-clad, underfed, and poorly equipped. They had only a vague idea—or none at all—of the issues for which they were asked to give their lives.

When the czarist government fell and subsequently the Provisional Government was established under the leadership of Alexander Kerensky of the Menshevik party, some of the soldiers merely dropped their arms and headed in the direction of their native villages. During the tumultuous period between the March revolution and the Bolshevik capture of state power in November, the number of desertions increased rapidly.

In addition to the chaotic military and political situations that existed during this period, living conditions had gone from bad to worse. The bread ration, which had been set at one pound a day in March, was reduced to three-quarters of a pound by October. Moreover, the cost of this most important item in the Russian people's diet doubled.

On the land, the peasants fought bitterly with the landlords over their threatened holdings. The peasants insisted that the land belonged to them, in the name of the mir. In fact, all during this difficult period, the mir, as the oldest established structure of orderly administration, regained much of its lost authority. In addition to battling with the landowners, the peasants fought the new government's decrees regarding landlord-peasant relationships, tax collectors, and food-supply committees that were trying to expedite food deliveries to the cities and the soldiers.

With the peasants in control of the source of the food, they held a club, in effect, at the head of the new government. Victor Chernov, a Socialist Revolutionary who had become Minister of Agriculture, had stated that "the peasantry is the real autocrat of Russia," and, in a sense, they were now a major force. All political factions made overtures to them for support—and for food. The peasants responded by withholding food deliveries, destroying property-line boundaries, appropriating cattle, and refusing to pay compensation for seized land. The Menshevik government made nationalization of land one of its policies. However, by its laxness in implementing its decision, the peasant resentment—and peasant seizure of land—increased. The fact that the government fixed prices for agricultural products but refused to do so for manufactured goods further infuriated the peasants. They were now caught in the familiar squeeze practiced so often by the previous government—high prices for manufactured items and low prices for agricultural products.

All during this period, Russia continued its role in the war. German naval detachments were moving closer to Petrograd (St. Petersburg). The government's announced intention of moving the capital to Moscow fed the rumors that it would surrender to the Germans. There were several disorders among Russian troops in Finland. An insurrection broke out in the Turkestan area. Army desertions increased tremendously, especially among those being sent to the front lines. It was estimated that three-quarters of the troops sent by Kerensky from Petrograd to the front had deserted. Many soldier units, through their representatives, were electing to support the Bolsheviks, who had raised the slogan of "Peace, Land, and Bread." The position of the Provisional Government, under the leadership of the Mensheviks, was rapidly becoming untenable.

Before dawn on November 7 (October 25, old calendar), 1917, troops led by the Bolsheviks captured the government headquarters at the Winter Palace in Petrograd and arrested the ministers, except Kerensky, who had left the previous day. The Provincial Government immediately came to an end. The Bolsheviks, under the leadership of Lenin, took power through the Congress of Soviets.

Among the first actions of the Congress when it met the next day were a resolution for peace and a decree on land. In moving for immediate action on the problems of land, the Bolsheviks were recognizing the absolute need to try to bring the peasantry over to its side. As John Reed pointed out in his book on the Russian revolution, *Ten Days That Shook the World:* "In the long run everything depended on the peasants. . . . The Bolsheviki had a comparatively small following among the peasants; and a permanent dictatorship of Russia by the industrial workers was impossible."

The decree on land abolished all private ownership of land without compensation to the landowners. All landowners' estates, including those of the crown and the church with all their buildings, livestock, etc., were transferred to the local township Land Committees and to the district Soviets of Peasants' Deputies until the meeting of the Constituent Assembly. Penalties were imposed for damage to confiscated property. Guidelines for administration were established according to instructions that had previously been published by the All-Russian Soviet of Peasants' Deputies. No lands of peasants and Cossacks serving in the army would be confiscated.

Actually, the decree on land did not incorporate the Bolshevik position that land would be nationalized. Instead, it provided that the local peasant bodies should decide the local form of land tenure. Each village was free to elect whether land tenure was to be by households, individuals, village communes, or cooperatives. In many ways, it resembled the position on land reforms advocated by the Socialist Revolutionaries.

The Bolsheviks realized, even then, that Lenin's concept of state farms and collective farms was not one that most peasants favored. The peasants had no experience with either form and wanted neither. These kinds of state control, except in a small percentage of the total arable land area, would have to wait for a future, more opportune, time to be put into effect on a large scale. What the Bolsheviks did, therefore, was to satisfy for the time being the peasants' age-old cry of "the land belongs to God and the people," and not to the state, even a Communist state.

The Bolsheviks had come to power with their slogan, "Peace, Land, and Bread." The Brest-Litovsk Treaty with Germany in March, 1918, gave the Russian people peace, at least with the Central Powers. The decree on land gave the peasants land. But there seemed nothing that the Communists could do to ensure bread for the people. As the months passed, food supplies became worse. All of life, it seemed, focused on the struggle to obtain food. A drought in 1920 heightened the extremely difficult food crisis that already existed. Food collectors sent by the government to the peasant areas were killed and uprisings occurred in several places. Petrograd was described as a city that was "grim . . . full of hunger, cold, and fear." Wealthier city people went to the villages and bartered expensive clothes, furniture, and jewelry for food, inasmuch as the peasant refused to take the paper money that had become worthless.

In addition to the shortage of food, the entire economy and standard of living declined. Locomotives did not operate because of a lack of fuel and spare parts. Oil wells and coal mines were idle. Medicine was almost nonexistent. Millions of demobilized peasants sought employment in the cities or returned to impoverished villages. Robber bands roamed the countryside. The famine of 1920–21 killed at least 3 million (some estimates were as high as 10 million), and malnutrition contributed to making many millions of others ill from a variety of diseases. Wild bands of deserted children roamed the cities. In some areas, cannibalism was reported.

In the midst of all this suffering, and contributing to it, was the civil war that broke out between the Reds (the Bolsheviks and their supporters) and the Whites (supporters of the former czar and other anti-Bolshevik forces). From 1918 to 1921, armies of the Bolsheviks fought those of the anti-Bolsheviks throughout a good part of Russia. Foreign intervention by troops, supplies, money, or all three against the Soviet government by a number of countries—including Japan, Germany, France, Britain, Czechoslovakia, Poland, and the United States—helped to prolong and intensify the war.

Some peasants supported the Reds, others supported the Whites, still others joined bandit groups that preyed upon both armies and civilians, and some remained uncommitted to any group. Actually during these years of War Communism, as the period of the civil war is known, many peasants were hardly conscious of the revolution and its issues. To them, their poverty and hunger hadn't changed at all from czarist days and, in fact, had become worse. They saw Reds kill Whites and Whites kill Reds with the peasants, as usual, suffering the greatest number of casualties. In the long run, however, the Bolshevik promise of land to the peasants without compensation to the landlord won over the support of most peasants. In the propaganda battle, as well as in the military struggle, the Reds were victorious.

However, the victory was a bitter one. Russia was prostrate. Industrial production had shrunk to about 13 percent of the 1913 volume. All phases of agriculture had declined. From 1916 to 1920, the number of horses, vital for farming, had declined from 31 million to 24 million. During the same period, the number of cattle was reduced from 50 million to less than 37 million. The harvest of grains was but a fraction of the pre-World War I total.

In many parts of Russia after the civil war, there were serious disturbances among the peasants and even, as at Kronstadt in 1921, among the sailors of the Red Navy. At the Communist

Party Convention of March, 1921, the situation was summarized by Lenin: "We are in a condition of such poverty, ruin, and exhaustion of the productive powers of the workers and peasants," he said, "that everything must be set aside to increase production."

This was the beginning of the New Economic Policy (NEP) that involved a fundamental change of policy with regard to both agriculture and industry. The tax structure on the peasant was changed, allowing him to retain more of his crop. In addition, he was now free to dispose of his surplus on the open market. Similar free-enterprise arrangements were made in industry. In a sense, a form of state capitalism was introduced.

On the land itself, many of the state farms and collectives that had been established during the period of War Communism were rented out or abandoned. The number of individual holdings increased. Stolypin's hope in the last years of czardom that Russia could become a nation of "strong and sober" farmers was being partially realized by the development of a fairly large number of richer peasants who took advantage of the freer economic system to hire other peasants and to increase their land holdings.

During the NEP, the government encouraged free enterprise in agriculture in order to increase production; yet at the same time it promoted, within limits, the idea of equalization of land holdings by continual redistribution of property to returning soldiers and others. On the whole, however, the NEP succeeded in raising production.

In 1927, the makeup of rural Russia consisted of the following: 3 percent of agricultural households were employed on state farms or collective farms. Eight percent of the peasants—the rural proletariat—hired themselves out to others for wages. About 20 percent worked part time on their own tiny holdings—up to three acres—and part time for others. About 65 percent of the peasants were middle farmers who produced enough for their own needs plus a small surplus with which to buy goods. These peasants numbered about 81 million persons and were the solid core of the peasantry. The small "capitalist" farmer, or kulak, represented about 4 percent of all peasants. Together with their families, they totaled about 5 million persons.

Throughout the NEP period, which lasted from 1921 to 1929, when the First Five-Year Plan was introduced, the peasant was used by those in power. By keeping industrial prices high and agricultural prices low, the ruling power could drain off the agricultural surplus to finance industry or other government projects. This exploitation of the peasant was a constant feature under czardom, War Communism, the NEP, and subsequently under the various five-year plans.

The peasant was still forced to pay a steep agricultural tax. Together with other taxes, he paid about 32 percent of his income in taxes. Industry, which had almost come to a standstill during the War Communism period, had to be rebuilt. It was the peasant production that had to do the job. As one observer noted: "It was the farm that paid the bills and received little or nothing in return in the way of manufactured goods." In fact, the taxes were so heavy that even the Communist party conference in 1926 concluded: "The attempt to regard the peasant merely as an object of taxation, in order by means of excessive taxes and the increasing of retail prices to raise exceptional capital from the farmer, must inevitably stop the progress of the productive power of the village, diminish the commodities of agriculture, and produce the menace of a rupture of the union of the working class and the farmer."

It is little wonder, therefore, that as late as 1929, some twelve years after the revolution, historian John Maynard could report that the peasant would say, "We are not Soviet people. We are peasants. . . ." This was not an expression of hostility, Maynard adds, but a plain statement of fact. Karl Borders, an American who was in Russia in the 1920s, wrote:

"What is the peasant's attitude toward the Communists? . . . [The peasant] likes that government best which interferes with him least. His general attitude toward the machinery of State is characterized by indifference and an inherited suspicion of all government. It is against this very wall of indifference that the Soviet state is battering by every effort to make the local machinery of government simple and realistically near the everyday life of the village. . . . Essentially conservative, imbedded in centuries of tradition and custom, and close to the elemental processes of nature that go on in spite of czars, war and revolutions, the peasant plants, depends on the weather, and reaps what God gives him. Experiments are made in government and in farming. He shakes his head, shrugs his shoulders, and waits."

During the 1920s, new agricultural arrangements and methods had made an appearance. One of these was the new agricultural communes, which had a tremendous growth right after the revolution. These had been organized on land that had been assigned to groups of workers by the new government. Equal sharing was the rule. All property was held in common. Work was assigned and performed according to each person's ability and skill. All income was held in common and goods were distributed according to each person's needs. Everyone ate together at a communal table. Every detail of life was discussed, from the washing of dishes to the building of a barn. Children were housed in common dormitories and cared for by members of the commune who were assigned to them.

Most of the communes were formed by ardent members of the Communist party or by its sympathizers. A few were organized by religious groups. More than two thousand were in existence by July 1919, but few of them survived the NEP period.

In addition to the communes, there were the *artels*. These were associations composed of peasants who pooled their work, animals, and machinery for the cultivation of land held in common. Each member lived in his own house, and there was no communal living. Each peasant had his share in the enterprise, and profits were divided on a proportionate basis. There were almost five thousand artels in existence in September 1920, but the number dropped severely during the NEP.

The agricultural cooperative, which had a rise in popularity in the years before the revolution, became quite popular during the NEP. These were similar in many respects to agricultural cooperatives in other countries. Farmers engaged in milk-producing, for instance, would join to buy grain, run a retail store, and market their product. In January 1927, there were about 30,000 cooperatives in the Soviet Union, with a constituency of nearly 7 million peasant families. After the period of the NEP, the traditional kind of cooperative began to disappear.

The two forms of agricultural organization developed during

this period that did not dwindle but increased were the state farms and the collective farms, which will be described later. However, it should be noted that many members of the defunct communes and artels of the 1920s found their way to these new farms, especially to the collective farms.

By the time the NEP gave way to the First Five-Year Plan in 1929, the peasants had lived for more than a decade of life under a different form of government. To all appearances, outward life was the same—with little or no change in living quarters, food, and dress. But attitudes were beginning to change in spite of the isolation of most peasant communities. The years of civil war had taken their toll, and many young peasants had become cynical and skeptical. There was an increase in early marriages, illegitimate births, abortions, venereal disease, and drunkenness. More and more youth resorted to civil marriages. What seemed most shocking to the American Quaker Karl Borders was the following report that he wrote in the mid-1920s:

> The social life of the young people remains simple, though an atmosphere of Main Street is beginning to appear here and there in the sections nearest the cities. . . . The importations from the West have included the shimmy and the fox-trot, and once, at a movie in Tsaritsyn, the orchestra in almost classic mood burst into what my startled ears were compelled to recognize as "Yes, We Have No Bananas." One shudders to think of what may happen if, or rather when, these concomitants of "civilization" fall upon the unsuspecting countryside of Russia.

19 The Drive Toward Collectivization

THE drive toward collectivization undertaken by the Soviet government in the late 1920s was destined to have the most profound impact on the peasants of any government action, whether by czars or commissars. Even emancipation, which legally freed the serf, had not resulted in a fundamental change in the life style of the peasant. He had remained poverty-stricken, isolated, uncultured, illiterate, and unassimilated into the mainstream of Russian society. The decision by the Communists to put the bulk of the peasants on collective farms eventually changed the peasant's relationship with the land, other peasants, the workers and intellectuals, and the government. Most importantly, it also eventually changed his style of living, cultural outlook, and political and social viewpoints.

By 1928, it had become clear to Russia's leader, Stalin, and to other leading members of the government and party that a socialized industrial system and an independent agricultural system

were incompatible. The NEP had given the Soviet state an economic breathing spell and had allowed both industry and agriculture to recover somewhat from the ravages of the civil war. Now
the Soviet leadership believed it was the time to move forward
with its plans for the socialization of all phases of the economy.

In the spring of 1928, the Central Committee of the Communist
Party decided to put into action a system of collective farming
throughout the Soviet Union. The government's first step was to
wipe out the independent, wealthier peasant—the kulak. In a series of actions, the government imposed heavy taxes, withdrew
his right to rent land, and expelled him from the mir. The kulak
and other peasants fought back by killing government agents who
had been sent into villages. They burned down properties of
various kinds and even engaged in small, pitched battles with the
authorities. The government struck back violently with wholesale
executions and banishments to Siberia. In the government's own
words, this was "ruthless class war" and a "socialist offensive on
all fronts."

In February 1930, a decree was issued in which a million kulaks
and their families were declared non-farmers and their possessions were confiscated. Komsomols (Young Communist Party
members), agents of the OGPU (the secret police), Communist
functionaries of various kinds, and worker brigades from the cities
descended upon the villages and farms, and by propaganda,
force, or a combination of both, succeeded in enlisting 55 percent
of the peasants into collective farms. However, many of these
farms existed only on paper or in elementary form and were unable to supply the nation with food. In an article entitled "Dizzy
with Success," Stalin put an end to this sham form of collectivization and called for a more organized drive to collectivize the peasants. Subsequently, the collective farms were favored with money,
equipment, and other advantages.

The reaction to the government's drive was met with resistance
not only from the kulaks but from other peasants, too. Many peasants killed their livestock to frustrate the government's demand
that the animals be transferred to the collectives. Some felt that
it was to their material advantage to get what they could for the
animals and thus share nothing with the collective farm. Many

peasants, now uprooted from their own land, wandered over Russia, trying to find a way to keep out of the collectives. Some of the opposing peasants were convinced by a steady stream of propaganda to join collectives; others were sent to Siberia; still others were killed.

The government had insisted that the bulk of the peasants should be on collective farms within a three-year period. To uproot an entire nation's peasants, transfer them to different kinds of agricultural and personal relationships, and establish a complete system of food production and distribution was a monumental task. The entire countryside was in turmoil. Nothing in Russia's past quite compared with it, not even the mass transfer of peoples so common in Russia from the days of Ivan the Terrible. Argument, persuasion, threat, force, and murder were all used to accomplish the mass transfer.

With this pressure, the government's drive was basically successful. By October 1930, 25 percent of agricultural Russia had been collectivized. A year later, the figure was 60 percent, with an even higher percentage in the more fertile areas. But the opposition to collectivization still continued, now from within the collectives as well as from without. Peasants were accused of stealing. Managers were fired or sent to Siberia because of personal profiteering. Collective-farm members stole grain and sold it for personal gain. "Kulak influences" were suspected in almost all phases of collective-farm life. The government sent special brigades to "supervise" the peasants. Communist party members were dispatched to oversee the farms and spot troublemakers. Members of a section of the secret police were assigned to the larger collective farms.

The kulak was tagged the class enemy of the entire Soviet society. Stalin called on the nation to "liquidate the kulak," who was pictured as a bloodsucking monster, a thief, a usurer, a murderer, an exploiter, and a parasite. In reading the literature of that period, it is almost impossible to believe that he was also a human being. In the 1880s, fifty years before these events, Stepniak, the Populist writer, had described the kulak thus:

> The kulaks are peasants who, by good luck or individual ability, have saved money and raised themselves above the common herd. This done, the way to further advancement is easy and rapid. They

want neither skill nor industry, only promptitude to turn to their profit the needs, the sorrows, the sufferings, and the misfortunes of others.

The great advantage the kulaks possess over their numerous competitors in the plundering of the peasants, lies in the fact that they are members, generally very influential members, of the village commune. This often enables them to use for private ends the great political power which the self-governing mir exercises over each individual member. The distinctive characteristics of his class are very unpleasant. It is the hard, pinching cruelty of a thoroughly uneducated man who has made his way from poverty to wealth, and has come to consider money-making, by whatever means, as the only pursuit to which a human being should devote himself. Kulaks, as a rule, are by no means devoid of natural intelligence and practical good sense.

Stepniak then noted that the peasant would rather go to the kulak for credit than to the landlord. He wrote: "The peasant dreaded the formalities, the documents, the legal tricks and cavils which the big people have in store for a benighted man and so would rather go to one of his own kind, who are peasants like himself."

The Communist government's bare-bones definition of the kulak was that he was a "peasant who systematically employs hired labor, who possesses power-driven machinery such as a flour-mill or a wool-combing machine, who hires out such machinery or contracts to work on other farms, who rents out living quarters, who leases land for commercial purposes, or who receives unearned income of any kind." It was, indeed, a definition that was so broad that were it employed, say, in the United States, the overwhelming majority of the farmers would be considered antigovernment.

The property of the kulaks was expropriated by the government and turned over to the collective farms. Eventually, it was estimated that 15 percent of the property of the collectives was derived from the kulaks.

The drive against the kulaks in which the government violated their personal and political rights was nothing new in Russian society. The government, whether czarist or Communist, demanded that the good of the state, as they viewed it, supersede the rights of the individual. This was true throughout the history of Russia, as far back as one can trace it as a state. The Communists did not invent the concept of the state's precedence over the individual. The Communists lifted it lock, stock, and barrel from their predecessors, the czars, as they lifted so many other facets of czarist rulership—the cry of foreign encirclement, political confessions of guilt, forced movements of people from their homes, exile to Siberia, adulation of a political father figure, and so forth. Forty years before the Russian revolution, D. Mackenzie Wallace wrote: "In all matters in which state interests are supposed to be involved, the rights of individuals are ruthlessly sacrificed."

The success of the government drive for collectivism was not only the result of propaganda and extremely forceful methods. It was also made possible because collectivization had its roots deep in the history and life of the Russian peasant for hundreds of years. In many ways, collectivization was not a revolutionary idea but an old one. There had always been a collectivistic streak in the Russian peasant, which accounted for his unique development of the mir. As one observer commented: "It [collectivism] hustled the peasants back into their age-old communes, where they rediscovered the equality of poverty and unfreedom and resumed their position as the lowest social estate."

Certainly, in the early days of the collective farms this was so. Stalin's emphasis on industrialization meant continuing poverty for the peasants, who through their sacrifices had to pay the tremendous cost of making Russia a modern industrial state. Under Stalin, the peasants were the most exploited class in the Soviet Union. In Marxist terms, the state expropriated from the peasants the surplus value of their labor as profit to finance Russia's frantic drive for industrialization.

The Communists had learned from the czar how to rule a state by elevating one class above another and by silencing the opposition. Thus, they elevated the workers above the peasants and silenced the kulaks. And they had learned from the capitalists how to extract profit from the labor of one social class to finance the goals of the state. Actually, this was not surprising, for the Communists never claimed to be egalitarians. They openly declared the workers to be superior to the peasants, if not as human beings then at least as political beings. For many years after the revolution and in various government bodies, the vote of a peasant representative was only a fraction—as little as one-fifth—of that of a representative of the workers. It wasn't until 1936 with the adoption of the new Soviet Constitution that the peasant was granted full political equality with the worker.

Lenin's insistence that the workers were the backbone of the new state—the dictatorship of the proletariat, as the Communists called it—was no idle remark. In the first decades of the new Russia, the peasant was an ally, not a co-ruler with the worker. In effect, he was a second-class citizen. And this meant that he had to bear the brunt of the many sacrifices and hardships that resulted from Russia's headlong plunge into twentieth-century industrialization.

20 The Collective and State Farm

EVER since the successful collectivization campaign of the early 1930s, almost all persons in the USSR who work in agriculture are members of either a collective farm or a state farm. Today, these two forms of agricultural organization account for approximately 97 percent of the arable land under cultivation in the country. The other 3 percent are the small individual garden plots tilled by the peasant near his house. The mir is gone completely and so is the new type of agricultural commune established after the revolution in which all persons shared all things in common.

In the *kolkhoz* (collective farm), the peasant household is no longer the basic farm unit. The kolkhoz deals with the individual peasant worker. The man or woman is entirely independent of the family in his or her work relations with the collective. The member of the collective farm is assigned to a work brigade, and the entire labor force of the collective is subdivided into these groups. For his work, the peasant is credited with a labor day, which represents the performance of specific work tasks. These labor days are then calculated in arriving at his income in kind or in cash.

The income of the farm worker depends on the income of the collective farm itself. If the particular farm is very productive and profitable, his income is higher than if he is a member of a less productive or profitable collective. Generally, payment for labor is determined in the following manner. The expenses of operating the farm, taxes, and money that is required for a fund that is nondistributable are subtracted from the gross income of the collective. The remainder is then divided by the total number of workday units performed. This determines an average payment per workday unit. The total payment to the peasant is obtained by multiplying the number of workdays by the average payment per workday. In some cases, this method has been superseded by a system in which payment is made for the actual day worked. Even so, the amount paid per day is dependent on the profit made by the collective for that year.

Collective farming. The woman on the left will receive grain crops in return for her work on the farm (1945).

Sovfoto

Modern harvesting techniques on a collective farm in 1971.

The farm land is the property of the state, although the members have the right to use it permanently. Each peasant household is permitted to have a plot of land for a garden, which it is allowed to consider its own. The size of these garden plots varies from one to five acres. On these plots, the peasant can raise fruits and vegetables or keep chickens or a cow. The produce from this plot belongs to him, and he can use it for his family or sell it on the open market.

Over the years, collectives have decreased in number but increased in size. In 1935, there were about 250,000 collective farms. By 1960, their number had been reduced to about 44,000 and by 1970 to approximately 35,000.

The five-year plans provide quotas for agricultural production as well as for industrial output. Overall agricultural quotas are set by the government's central planning group based on individual collective farm and state farm capabilities throughout the nation. Tremendous pressure is exerted through exhortation and penalties for each farm to meet its quotas. Outstanding producers are given special consideration and individuals are decorated and given rewards. Details of farm management are handled by the general meeting of the collective. This meeting resembles to an extent those of the old mir, with the farm chairman taking the place of the village elder. The chairman is usually appointed by the government, although in recent years he could be elected by the members with government approval. In many cases, especially in the early years of the new regime, the chairman was a political appointee and had little knowledge of local conditions. The novels of Mikhail Sholokhov, such as *Seeds of Tomorrow,* and those of Maurice Hindus describe in dramatic terms the struggle between such politically motivated chairmen and peasants on the collective farms.

The chairman is not the only bureaucrat or nonfarming member of the collective. There are also auditors, bookkeepers, doctors, and others who perform various functions related to the productivity and welfare of the collective.

There is firm discipline. For disturbing the order of the collective, a peasant may be punished by fines, demotion in the kind of work he is asked to perform, and in extreme cases by expulsion from the farm.

Throughout the establishment and development of the collective farm system, the Soviet government was unwilling to trust the farm members to manage their own affairs without Communist party supervision. Although this has been relaxed in recent years and there has been some decentralization of authority, the government still maintains a tight control through its central planning, taxation, and political appointees.

Mechanization of farm production has increased tremendously under the new system. Almost from the beginning of the new agricultural system soon after the revolution, there was a drive by the government to mechanize agriculture. In the early years when industrial production in Russia was so backward, there was little, if any, manufacture of such vital equipment as tractors. As early as 1919, when the Commissar of Agriculture was asked by a foreign correspondent, Arthur Ransom, what he regarded as the greatest need of agricultural Russia, he made a one-word reply: "Tractors." Karl Borders reported that when he was in Russia in 1922 as a relief worker with the Quakers, a commune member said: "We don't believe in God any longer. The tractor is our god." The tractor became a symbol for progress on the farm. Throughout the countryside there were posters with pictures of tractors on them and tractors were even engraved on paper money. In the early 1920s, the Soviet Commissar of Agriculture observed:

"The tractor is of extreme importance for collectivization. . . . The tractor, without doubt, is one of the greatest factors in eliminating the lines of individual peasant production. If a tractor is linked with the cooperative and is used correctly, we have in it not only an agricultural machine but a new factor in the growth of the socialist element in the village. The tractor unites the poor peasants particularly, raising their production, and in a real way preventing the kulak from exploiting them. It allows them to put up a real fight with the capitalistic element in the village."

In 1925, ten thousand tractors, built by the Ford Motor Company, were imported. Within a short time, because of poor handling and lack of spare parts, most of them remained idle in the villages. As late as 1926, Russia had only one domestic factory, the Putilovski, producing tractors. With the First Five-Year Plan, the production of tractors and other mechanized equipment was given high priority. Subsequently, thousands of tractors poured off the assembly lines.

Over the years, an increasing number of Machine Tractor Stations (MTS) were established all over the Soviet Union and became a feature on collective farms. The farms rented the equipment and paid for it with a percentage of their produce. The tractor driver himself became a kind of folk hero, celebrated in novels and movies of the period. Probably more than any other single factor, the tractor—and mechanization in general—changed agriculture in Russia from one of the most backward to one of the

A woman and her tractor in the early days of collectivization.

most advanced systems. In recent years, the MTS have been largely superseded by farms that own their own equipment.

The eight thousand state farms that exist in the Soviet Union account for almost half of the nation's cultivated area. Originally formed from estates that had been taken over by the government and operated by an agricultural trust, they now form one of the two main agricultural mechanisms in the Soviet state. Usually larger than a collective farm, the *sovkhoz* (state farm) sometimes is a gigantic enterprise consisting of tens of thousands of acres and huge investments in buildings and machinery. In addition to raising crops, state farms are used to breed horses and as areas for the raising of cattle, sheep, and pigs as well as fur-yielding animals.

On the state farms, the peasant is a wage-earning worker in much the same way as a worker in a factory. The sovkhoz is completely owned and operated by the government. Many of them employ thousands of workers, with the average being about eight hundred workers. Work is on a year-round basis and wages are not determined by the profit of the farm, as in the case of the collec-

Russian farm workers: (above) *on the farm;* (below) *at the market.*

tives, but by a set wage according to the kind of job that is performed.

The state farm worker has his own individual house and vegetable garden. As is the case with the collective farm worker, the worker on the state farm devotes a good deal of his time and effort to cultivating his own garden. In 1963, he was forbidden to have his own private livestock.

There have been many cases in which a collective farm was not profitable and the government made arrangements to transform it into a state farm. Many observers of Soviet agricultural organization believe that it will only be a question of time before all agriculture in Russia will be under the supervision of state farms.

Russian observers themselves seem to feel that the management of state farms is often superior to that of the collectives and, as a result, they are more efficient and workmanlike. Vladimir Soloukhin, in his book *A Walk in Rural Russia,* compared the forests that were run by collectives and those run by the state:

Soviet dairymaids.

Sovfoto

Anyone who has walked in forests at all will immediately distinguish kolkhoz forest from state forest. Kolkhoz forest is cluttered up; twigs, broken boughs and tree-tops lie rotting on the ground . . . extraordinarily high stumps stick up on all sides . . . then there are decaying trees . . . trees are felled at random, without any system, and the young growth is not cut down. . . .

On the other hand when you go into a state forest, you seem to be entering a well-tended room; here there is space, beauty and splendour. Branches do not lie around where they have fallen but are stacked in neat piles, ready for burning or carting away. You will not see tall stumps, but if there are any stumps at all, they are on a clearing where all the trees have been felled. The empty spaces are planted with young trees, set in straight lines.

After more than fifty years, certain errors that were made in early years are still being repeated, forcing many persons to wonder if certain kinds of mistakes are not inherent in the Soviet system of agriculture itself. For example, a dispatch in May 1970, from American newspaper correspondent Ray Vicker, noted that "sometimes machinery is dispatched late to farms. Fertilizer may pour in carloads to certain farms, while others wait vainly for supplies. Communist party bigwigs sometimes dictate farm plans without understanding local conditions; pricing set by planners may be arbitrary."

In general, agriculture has not kept pace with the advances in industry. The agricultural quotas were not realized in several of the five-year plans. So-called scientific advances in agriculture have often proven to be less than advances and have not been advantageous to crop yields. In some cases, new crops or methods were introduced on a large scale without proper testing, and they proved to be failures. As late as 1969, the gross farm output was 3 percent less than the previous year. The Five-Year Plan of 1965–1970, which was supposed to produce an increase of 25 percent, was not fulfilled. "Agriculture lags behind industry everywhere as regards the rate of growth," the Soviet economist Stanislav Strumilin complained in 1970. In the same year, Leonid Brezhnev, the Communist party leader, also noted that there were many agricultural failures, specifically mentioning shortages of eggs, meat, and milk.

Novosti from Sovfoto

Mechanized tea harvesting on a state farm, 1971.

In spite of many problems—both old and new—the new Soviet system of agriculture has improved the condition of the peasant in many respects. However, the distance between availability and fulfillment of individual wants is as great in Russia as it is in other countries. Millions of individual peasants do not, and in some cases cannot, take advantage of the new worlds that have been opened to them. The poor peasant, of which there are many in Russia, still does not have all the advantages of the better-off peasant, worker, intellectual, or party member. Those in isolated geographic areas still must suffer their isolation from cultural centers. The rebel, the iconoclast, the naysayer, and the critic of the political system have no easier time now than in the days of the czar. The distance to Siberia is still the same.

21 The New Soviet Peasant

MORE than half a century has elapsed since the Russian Revolution of 1917. Has the new Soviet system produced a new Soviet man and specifically a new Soviet peasant? Great changes have occurred everywhere during the past five or six decades in politics, economics, science, technology, medicine, education, transportation, communication, agriculture, and a host of other areas. Allowing for these changes, is the Russian peasant today a different person from his forebears? Has he changed significantly and fundamentally or is he basically the same peasant merely living under a different political system?

These questions have been raised since the beginning of the Soviet regime by those who would justify and defend the new system of government and by those who would condemn and attack it. Hundreds of books and thousands of articles have been printed and innumerable discussions have raged, not only on the subject of communism as a political system but whether or not it would create a "new Soviet man." Even those who are sympathetic to the Soviet system concede that though there have been revolutionary changes in almost all phases of man's life in the Soviet Union, the fundamental nature of man himself is too complex to admit of absolute answers to the questions. In other words, the frailties of the human being, his ambitions, his drive for power, his intimate personal life, and his concern for political freedom, social equality, and the right of independent expression of opinion are aspects of man's makeup that admit of no absolute and definitive judgments and conclusions. At best, the so-called better life is an aspiration to strive toward. At worst, political rigidity, ideological dogma, and personal privilege and power constantly work against this striving to achieve a noble, unselfish, full, and free life for all the people.

Jessica Smith, a Soviet defender for many years, observed on the fiftieth anniversary of the revolution that she had asked the question about the "new Soviet man" as long as forty years ago. She noted that she is still asking the question about the emergence of such a man and wrote:

> You hear a great deal today about the training and development of "the new Soviet man," recognized as the most important and difficult task of all in the transition to communism. "What is this new Soviet man? What are his qualities, his aspirations?" I asked everywhere. There were many answers. "A person of great moral purity"; "a seeker of knowledge, of many-sided attainments, advancing side by side with others, never at their expense"; "man to man must be a friend, comrade and brother"; "a person of boundless romanticism, striving for heroic deeds"; "what we seek is to learn everything we can, to face any hardship, to be ready for any sacrifice, to work for better lives for ourselves and the whole collective. . . .
>
> I wrote of things like this over forty years ago and believed them to be true. . . . Building socialism turned out to be a bigger and longer task than any of us dreamed of. . . . There are all kinds of people in the Soviet Union. Good people and bad people, bureaucrats and dogmatists, careerists and self-seekers as well as heroes. But everywhere, you see this new Soviet man emerging. No one claims he has achieved all these qualities as yet, but they are already discernible."

Stephen and Ethel Dunn in their book on the Russian peasant

sum up their thoughts on the peasant as he exists now, after a half-century under the Soviet regime: "The main fact about the Russian peasant is that after nearly fifty years of revolution, civil and international war, shoving and hauling, and superhuman effort and sacrifice, he remains a man in transition.

Professor Zbigniew Brzezinski, of Columbia University and director of its Research Institute on Communist Affairs, observed in March 1970, in an article in *Encounter* magazine, that all was not well with either the Soviet economy with respect to agriculture or with the Soviet peasant himself. "Soviet backwardness is particularly evident in agriculture," he wrote. "Agricultural productivity has leapfrogged during the last several decades in most developed countries and lately even in a number of the underdeveloped ones. No so in the Soviet Union, where productivity steadily declined and only recently has somewhat risen. The Soviet rural population is underemployed, undercompensated, and underproductive."

A number of observers feel that the collectives and the state farms have solved many of the age-old problems of Russian agriculture and peasant drudgery, although many farms are still not as productive, say, as those in advanced Western countries. The farmers on them have not achieved an enviable standard of living. The reasons are many.

Rural life in comparison to city life is dull and backward. The flight of the peasant to the city has increased over the past few decades. In the half-century since the revolution, the number of peasants in rural areas has decreased from 90 percent to less than 40 percent of the population. The village in Soviet Russia still resembles the village in the days of the czar. Fifty years or so after Gorky's description of the czarist village, which was previously quoted, Wright Miller's description of the Soviet village is strikingly similar:

> So they straggle, the Russian villages. . . . The fear of fire overcomes the native liking for community, and the little izbas are spaced far apart, four times their own width, along the great green tracks. With their doll-size gardens no larger than the huts themselves, their unpainted logs cracked and seamed by frost and sun, and their only decoration the fretted eaves which fringe roofs and tiny windows like

wooden lace, the older huts would seem, if they stood alone, fit scenes for some uncheerful fairy tale. But they repeat and repeat, facing each other across huge tracks that put the whole village even more out of scale.

In many a village there is no natural centre, not even a muddy space by the church. The village market is strung along a patch of dirt road, where women and children stand patiently or squat, offering a chicken, a paper of green tobacco, wild berries by the tumblerful, and drinks of kvas. . . . Under centuries of serfdom the village meeting gathered in the open air, and there was little incentive to make a communal centre or to leave any communal mark upon the settlement. And today the school or "cooperative" store or village Soviet, if there is such a building, is often just a larger hut somewhere in the general straggle. The emptiness among the houses and the wearisome scattering—they intensify one's impression of the diffuseness, the elusiveness, and the inaccessibility of Russia, to a degree which lavish peasant hospitality can never quite remove.

The Russian writer Vladimir Soloukhin, who toured the rural areas observed, too, that the Russian village under the Soviet government is still isolated and depressed. He quotes an old villager:

This was a village of carpenters. All of the men went off to Moscow, Petersburg, or somewhere. Only the women remained behind, and they didn't bother with gardens or orchards. They brought potatoes, onions, cucumbers, and other vegetables from the market in Pokrov. To tell the truth, the people were spoiled, they had rubles sent them from outside, and didn't need to work the land. Well, after the revolution, all the carpenters settled for good in Moscow. Each of them had some attachment there; besides they were frightened by tales of the expropriation of the wealthy peasants. So half the village ceased to exist. Nowadays the young people go away to school. Very few people are left, very few!

Soloukhin also points out that many peasants leave the villages and farms for more steady earnings in the cities. "In the country," one peasant explained, "you may work for a whole year, and it is not certain what you will receive at the end of it." Soloukhin explained to him that things have changed and that monthly advances are being paid on the collective farms. "We had heard rumors of it," the peasant replied. "If things are like that, of course we would go back. But otherwise, why work for nothing?"

Other observers have also pointed out the low earnings of peasants on collectives. Economist D. Gale Johnson, writing in *The Bulletin of the Atomic Scientists,* observed: "One of the major limitations of the collective farm system is the very tenuous connection between effort and reward for the individual member of the farm." Journalist Ray Vicker noted in a Moscow dispatch in 1970 that the productivity of the collective and state farms had not increased according to quotas formulated in the most recent Five-Year Plan. "Western sources attribute troubles to lethargic attitudes of farm workers, too. With no direct interest in farms, workers do what they are told and nothing more, preferring to devote careful attention to the private plots allocated them."

The old-time peasant family life has been severely shaken and in many ways has been shattered. The wife has now become a full-fledged worker and has put away the loom and the spinning wheel. One peasant custom after another has largely disappeared or become minimized. The youth leave for the more exciting life in the cities, and the influence of their elders over them has been greatly reduced.

Even in such traditional matters as weddings, customs have changed, although some of the trappings are still observed. The matchmaker is no more. There is no longer the ritual exchange of gifts, the elaborate ceremonial trips to and from the huts of the parents, the bride's party, the paying of a dowry, the inspection of the bride's family as a means of showing its wealth, and dozens of other customs. Some of the ritual is still observed but usually in a tongue-in-cheek manner. Few peasants are married in a church.

It is not surprising that extremely personal matters such as weddings should now be conducted differently. It would be surprising if they had remained the same, for the relationship of the Soviet peasant woman to the peasant man has changed considerably. The peasant woman is no longer a half slave to her husband, subject to whippings when she disobeys. She has become emancipated in almost all respects.

In the most remote areas, and even among the Muslims, women have gained full stature and respect. The centuries-old submissive female has disappeared together with the patriarchal male.

Women work side by side with men on the collectives and state farms, and their earnings are the same as the men's for equal work. All sorts of arrangements are made, such as day-care centers for the children, so that she can have her own economic existence, separate from that of her husband. For the first time in Russian history, she has an independence in the conduct of her personal life.

As a result, women have a predominant position in the life of the collectives and state farms. Many of them hold responsible jobs in the managerial and scientific aspects of the farm. One observer after another has maintained that in many ways women are the backbone of the collectives and state farms.

However, certain problems have not been solved, mainly the demands of motherhood and the carrying out of household chores. Despite day-care centers and other aids, the peasant woman, in reality, must not only be a full-time worker but still must look after her children to a large extent and do her own household work. This has resulted in fewer women than men being able to qualify for highly skilled and complex jobs, thus reducing her earning capacity.

The liberation of the peasant woman, and of women in general, has also freed her from many of the personal restrictions that were imposed upon her by official decree, custom, and superstition. She is free to marry whom she pleases and to have her marriage easily dissolved if it is unsatisfactory. However, the puritanical nature of Bolshevism is hostile to moral laxity. Officially at least, if not in practice, a strict moral code is advocated, with the sanctity of the family paramount in the order of things in Soviet life.

The strict code of conduct advocated by the Communists has replaced to some extent the influence of the church. The free love and sexual license that critics of the Communist regime predicted would occur had only a brief existence in the early days after the revolution. As the Soviet state solidified its hold on the people, it also strengthened its demands that persons live a well-ordered, well-disciplined life. In fact, today in the Soviet Union there is probably less so-called moral depravity and "loose living" than in the countries of the Western world.

Formal religion and the influence of the church are negligible. The supposed iron-clad attachment of the peasant to religion that some persons insisted could not be broken is no longer much in evidence. One observer of the present-day peasant has noted that "the parish priest is today rare; in his stead the collective farm chairman sits in the midst of the villagers."

Together with the disappearance of the parish priest and the village church, the overwhelming illiteracy of the peasant has also vanished. With its literacy rate at 95 percent of the population, Russia now ranks as one of the most advanced countries in the world in this respect. Schooling is now available for all persons. The peasant has the opportunity not only to attain a secondary-school education but to enroll in one of the country's forty-three universities. The peasant's sons and grandsons—and daughters—can aspire to be doctors, scientists, or politicians or elect to work in agriculture. Although the number of sons and daughters of peasants at the universities is less than that of the working class, the intellectuals, or the bureaucracy, the relative enrollment of peasants in centers of higher education far exceeds that which existed in czarist days.

Collective farm workers attend a literacy class.

Sovfoto

The wide cultural gap between city and village has been narrowed, though by no means abolished. Books, movies, radio, and television have brought the world closer to the peasant. He is no stranger to museums, if he lives within a reasonable distance of a city in which they are available. Traveling troupes of players and musicians tour the rural areas. The peasant himself, especially those who are better off economically, can now be seen as tourists in various parts of the country.

Nevertheless, there is this gap between city and country, and in some places it is still a wide one and the cultural life of the peasant has not changed appreciably. In fact, with the disappearance of the church, these isolated peasants have lost even the color, music, and drama of church ritual. The clubs of the collective farm, where they do exist in the more remote areas, are drab substitutes for the colorful churches.

With the great emphasis on production and meeting of farm quotas, the clubs—usually the only gathering place for those on the collective—have become centers for political propaganda. Soloukhin described one such club in the Vladimir district:

The walls, which were stained and cracked, were hung with posters so commonplace that no one would read them, or if by some chance anyone's glance fell on them, he would not pay the slightest attention to them. For example: "Let us take part in socialist competition! Let us finish the spring sowing campaign in the best agro-technical time!" In the first place, this poster evidently remained there in spring, summer, autumn, and winter, awaiting the next spring sowing campaign. Secondly, it is hard to imagine that a kolkhoz lad, having read such a slogan, would snatch up his cap and hurry away to take part in socialist competition. The truth must be admitted: people are profoundly indifferent to such visual propaganda.

(Left *and* Below) *The Russian peasant, old and new.*

UN photos

In terms of the day-to-day details, the life of the Soviet peasant is not radically different from that of his father or grandfather in czarist days. Like most people in most countries, the kinds of food that are appealing remain quite constant over the years. The Soviet peasant still relies heavily upon bread, potatoes, sauerkraut, pickles, dairy products, and fish. Meat is still in short supply. The basic difference—and an important one—is that the quantity of food has increased. The famines so common in the days of the czar, the early days of the new state, and the bitter famine of 1931–32—when the liquidation of the kulaks combined with a drought condemned millions of peasants to starvation and death—are no more.

The former holiday fare is seen more often, and peasant dishes such as jellied meat, baked sweet pudding made from cereal, meat turnovers, and Russian cheesecake are now on the tables more often. In some areas, the peasant has added more sophisticated fare such as vegetable salad, sausages, schnitzel, and pasta.

Although the wearing of Western-style clothing has increased, especially among the young people, the old-fashioned peasant costumes are still in evidence. Girls are seen more often in skirts and blouses, and more and more ready-made one-piece dresses are worn. Women still wear their kerchiefs and men their caps. The rags that so often passed for clothing in the old days are gone. However, the dress of the peasants, except on holidays, is still drab and old-fashioned.

Housing has improved for some peasants, although the old-time izba is still in evidence. Within the houses themselves, some comforts of modern-day living have been added. Manufactured goods, conspicuous by their absence in the peasant houses of old Russia, are making their appearance in more houses and in more variety. In some of the new houses, the entrance that leads to the living quarters is off the street while the entrance to the court is off the kitchen area. Shortage of widespread good housing is as much a problem for the Soviet peasant in the country as it is for the Soviet worker in the city.

Materially, the peasant is better off now than he was in the days of the old regime. For a group of millions of persons who suffered debt and hunger for centuries, this is no mean advancement.

Politically, the peasant has taken his place alongside the other main elements of the population—the worker and the intellectual. His second-class citizenship, carried over from czarist days to the early decades of Communist rule, is gradually lessening and, according to some observers, is no longer in evidence. The lack of political freedom that exists in the Soviet Union affects him equally but no longer specially.

Creatively, the outburst of energy that the revolution unleashed was made possible by the offspring of peasants as well as others in the population. Large numbers of peasants, both on and off the farms, are no longer visible as the backward, illiterate creatures without bread, without land, without culture, and without hope.

The peasant, like the worker, is the new Soviet man, in whatever way and by whatever definition one wants to measure him.

Bibliography
A selected list of Books in English

Baring, Maurice. *The Russian People*. London: Methuen, 1911.

Black, C. E., ed. *The Transformation of Russian Society*. Cambridge: Harvard University Press, 1960.

Blum, J. *Lord and Peasant in Russia from the 9th to the 19th Century*. Princeton, N.J.: Princeton University Press, 1961.

Borders, Karl. *Village Life Under the Soviets*. New York: Vanguard, 1927.

Dunn, S. P. and E. *The Peasants of Central Russia*. New York: Holt, Rinehart & Winston, 1967.

Haxthausen, A. F. L. M. *The Russian Empire*. London: Chapman & Hall, 1856.

Hindus, Maurice. *Broken Earth*. New York: International Publishers, 1926.

———.*Red Bread*. New York: Cape & Smith, 1931.

Koslow, Jules. *The Kremlin*. New York: Nelson, 1958.

———. *Ivan the Terrible*. London: W. H. Allen, 1961.

Kravchinski, S. M. [Stepniak]. *The Russian Peasantry*. New York: Harper, 1888.

Leroy-Beaulieu, A. *The Empire of the Tsars and the Russians*. New York: Putnam, 1894–96.

Mandel, W. *Russia Re-Examined*. New York: Hill & Wang, 1964.

Maynard, John. *The Russian Peasant and Other Studies*. London: Gollanez, 1942.

Miller, Wright. *The Russians as People*. New York: Dutton, 1961.

Palmer, F. *Russian Life in Town and Country*. New York: Putnam, 1901.

Poole, Ernest. *The Village: Russian Impressions*. New York: Macmillan, 1918.

Reed, John. *Ten Days That Shook the World*. New York: Modern Library, 1935.

Robinson, G. T. *Rural Russia Under the Old Regime*. London: Longmans, Green, 1932.

Sholokhov, Mikhail. *Seeds of Tomorrow*. New York: Knopf, 1935.

———.*Virgin Soil Upturned*. London: Putnam, 1935.

Tikhomirov, L. A. *Russia Political and Social*. London: Sonnenschein, 1892.

Troyat, H. *Daily Life in Russia Under the Last Tsar*. New York: Macmillan, 1962.

Vakar, N. *The Taproot of Soviet Society*. New York: Harper, 1962.

Venturi, F. *Roots of Revolution*. London: Weidenfeld, 1960.

Volin, L. "The Peasant Household Under the Mir and Kolkhoz in Modern Russian History," in Ware, C. R., ed., *The Cultural Approach to History*. New York: Columbia University Press, 1940.

Vucinich, W. S., ed. *The Peasant in Nineteenth-Century Russia*. Stanford, Calif.: Stanford University Press, 1968.

Wallace, D. MacKenzie. *Russia*. New York: Holt, 1881.

Williams, Harold W. *Russia of the Russians*. New York: Scribner, 1916.

Index

Agrarian reform groups, 115–116
Agriculture/agricultural
  collectivization of, 137–139
  crops, 43, 44
  growing season, 2
  mechanization of, 144
  production quotas, 143–144, 149
  systems, 37
  tools, 36, 42
Alexander I, 101
Alexander II, 102, 117
All-Russian Peasants Union, 121
Animals, farm, 7, 44
Arbiters of the Peace, 108
Army. See Military
Astrakhan, 77
Avvakum, Archpriest, 88

Baba-yaga, 91
Bania, 67
Bannik, 91
Barin, Maurice, 85

Barschina, 30, 45
Bath, steam, 66–67
Batraki, 32
Beggars, 57–58
Bering Strait, 1
Birukoff, Paul von, 8
Bolshevik party, 117, 120
  takes power, 126
Borders, Karl, 132, 134, 145
Bread, 63, 119
  rationing of, 127
Brest-Litovsk Treaty, 129
Brezhnev, Leonid, 149
Brzezinski, Zbigniew, 155
Bulavin, Kondratii, 76, 77
Bunin, Ivan, 35

Cannibalism, 130
Catherine II (the Great), 2, 5, 22, 27,
  41, 77, 101
Cattle, 37, 44
Census of 1858, 19

Chantreau (eighteenth-century Frenchman), 9, 42, 63
Chekhov, Anton, 23, 35, 72
Chernov, Victor, 127
Cherry Orchard, The (Chekhov), 72
Chicherin, B. N., 15
Chief Committee for Peasant Affairs, 102
Child labor, 98
Children, peasant, 53
Christianity, Russian, 90
Church, Orthodox, 86–88
    influence of, 159
    serfs owned by, 24
Civil rights, 106
Civil war, 130
Clergy, village, 85–87
Climate, 2
Clothing, 162
Code of 1649, 30
Collectives/collectivism, 89, 141–146
Commerce, peasants in, 41
Commune(s), 11, 105, 115, 123; *see also* Mir
    land distribution of, 37
    loss of power, 124
Communist(s), 54, 74
    code of conduct, 158
Communist Party, Central Committee of, 136
Congress of Soviets, 128
Conscription, army, 46–48, 59
Constantine, Grand Duke, 102
Constitution, Soviet, 140
Cossacks, Don, 77
Craven, Elizabeth, 66, 79
Crimean War, 102
Crops, 43, 44
Crown peasants, 4
Cruelty to peasants, 59

Dallas, George M., 98
Death

peasant concept of, 67–68
    rate, 60
Diary of a Writer (Dostoevsky), 81
Diderot, D., 27
Dnieper River, 2
Doctors, 60
Domovoi, 91
Don Cossacks, 77
Dostoevsky, Feodor, 35, 72, 81, 88
Dress, peasant, 64–65
Drink, 64
Dukhobory, 88, 89
Duma, Third, 124
Dunn, Ethel, 154
Dunn, Stephen, 154
Dvor, 11
Dvorovoi, 91

Economy, 129
Education, peasant, 60, 110
Emancipation of peasants, 101–103
    opponents of, 103
    law for, 105, 107
Exile, 95

Factory
    labor, peasant, 96–97
    system, spread of, 40
    working conditions, 98
Family, peasant, 67
    head of, 50–51
Famine, 162
    of 1891-92, 57, 120
    of 1920-21, 129
Farm(s)
    animals, 44
    collective, 131, 136–137, 141–146
    income, 142
    mechanization of, 144
    production quotas, 149
    vehicles, 43
Feasts, 37–38, 63
Feldsher, 60

Five-year plans, 132, 134, 149
Fletcher, Giles, 57, 79
Food, 63–64, 119, 162
   shortages, 129
Footwear, peasant, 65
Forced labor, 45
Ford Motor Company, 145
Funerals, 68

Gautier, Theophile, 95
Godunov, Boris, 3–4
Gogol, Nikolai, 23, 85
Gorky, Maxim, 35, 73
Great Novgorod, 2, 95
Great Russia, 24

Hairstyles, peasant, 66
Handicrafts, peasant, 39
   cooperatives, 39–40
Harvest, 37
Haxthausen, Baron, 15, 63, 80, 93
Haymaking, 37
Hindus, Maurice, 144
Horses, farm, 44
Hospitality, peasant, 62
House serfs, 4
Houses, peasant, 7–9, 162
House of the Dead, The (Dostoev-
   sky), 88
Hunger, 57

Icons, 9
Illiteracy, 60
Income, peasant, 44, 157
Industrialization, 99
Irrigation, 44
Iusupov, Prince, 19
Ivan the Great, 2, 3
Ivan the Terrible, 2, 32, 93, 94
Izba, 7

Johnson, D. Gale, 157
Justice, prerevolutionary, 59

Kabala, 46
Karamzin, Nicholas, 104
Kerensky, Alexander, 126
Khan, Genghis, 2
Khlysty, 88
Khozain, 11, 49, 54
Kiev, 2
Kluchevsky, Vasili, 23
Kolkhoz, 141
Komsomols, 136
Konyushennik, 91
Kovalevsky, N. N., 110
Kronstadt, 130
Kropotkin, Prince, 104
Kulaks, 32, 131, 136, 138
Kvas, 64

Labor
   child, 98
   forced, 45
   migrant, 119
Ladoga, Lake, 2
Land
   apportionment of, 12, 13–14, 109,
     119
   in communes, 12, 37
   nationalization of, 128, 129
Landowners, absentee, 28
Laws, 3, 59
Legislative Commission of 1767, 41
Legras, Jules, 95
Lenin, Nikolai, 117, 128
Leshii, 90
Leskov, N. S., 67

Machine Tractor Stations (MTS),
   145
Malnutrition, 130
Manufacturing, peasants in, 40
March Revolution, 126
Marriage, peasant, 30, 51, 54, 69
Marxists, 117

Matushka, 51

Maynard, John, 74, 132

Medicine, 60

Menshevik party, 120, 126

Merchants, peasant, 40

Migrant labor, 119

Migration
  government policy on, 95
  seasonal, 93

Military service
  desertions from, during revolution, 128
  peasants in, 46–48, 59, 75

Miller, Wright, 155

Mining, peasants in, 40

Mir, 11, 127
  autonomy of, 17
  critics of, 17
  economics of, 18
  origin of, 15–16

Molokane, 88, 89

Monomakh, Prince Vladimir, 22

Moscow, founding of, 2

Mother, peasant, 51

Narodnaya Volya, 116

Narodniki (Populists), 114

Nesselrode, Count, 103

New Economic Policy, 131

Nicholas I, 101

Nikhon, Patriarch, 88

Nizhni Novgorod (Gorki), 77, 86

Nicholas II, 59

Nobles
  crimes against serfs, 27
  as fops, 22–23
  in government, 22
  French-speaking, 22
  impoverished, 21
  serf ownership of, 19–20
  wealth of, 21

Nobles' Land Bank, 108

Novgorod, 2, 95

Obrok, 3, 30, 45

Obschina, 11

October Revolution, 126

Oka River, 2

Old Believers, 77, 85, 88

On the Russian Peasantry (Gorky), 35

Oppression of peasants, 34–35, 59, 78

Pastures, common, 7

Patriarchy, 33

Paul I, 76, 101

Peasant(s). *See also* Serfs
  adultery, 70
  appearance of, 66
  attitude to communism, 132
  character, 34, 74
  children, 53
  civil rights, 106
  communities, 11
  concept of death, 67–68
  crown, 4, 32
  cruelty to, 59
  cultural deprivation of, 110, 160
  death rate, 60
  debts of, 46
  diet of, 63–64
  dress, 64–65
  drinking habits, 79–80
  education, 60, 110
  emancipation, 101–103
  factory labor, 96–97
  family, 67, 157
  fatalism of, 75
  footwear, 65
  hairstyles, 66
  handicrafts, 39
  health of, 60
  hospitality, 62
  houses, 7–9
  illiteracy, 60, 159
  immobility, 92

inclination to lie, 81–82
income, 44, 157
indolence, 82
laws dealing with, 59
marriage, 51
-master relationship, 59
merchants, 40
migration, seasonal, 93
in military, 46–48, 59, 75
in mining and manufacturing, 40
mother, 51
obligations to landowners, 30
oppression, 34–35, 59, 78
population, 31, 60
poverty, 42, 56, 110
revolts, 76, 78, 101
rich, 32, 125
runaway, 76, 94, 95
sentenced to exile, 95
superstitions, 72, 90
view of life, 35
women, 51–52
Peasants' Land Bank, 124
Pech, 7
Peddlers, itinerant, 65
Peter the Great, 2, 3, 5, 22, 32, 92
Pilniak, Boris, 72
Plows, 42
Polevik, 90
Political parties, 115–117
Poole, Ernest, 80
Population, peasant, 60
Populists, 114–116
Potemkin, Prince, 25
Poverty, 42, 56, 110
Priest, village, 68, 86–87
Prostitutes, serfs as, 25
Provisional Government, 126, 128
Pskov, 95
Pugachev, Emelian, 76–78, 101

Quitrent, 3

Radziwill, Prince, 26
Railroad system, 95
Rainfall, 44
Ransom, Arthur, 145
Rasputin, Grigori, 89
Razin, Stenka, 76
Razumovski, Field Marshal, 25
Reed, John, 128
Reformers, 114
Religion/religious, 85, 159
    paintings, 9
    sects, 77, 87
Revolts, peasant, 76, 78, 101
Revolution
    of 1905, 120, 122–123
    of 1917, 54, 80, 126
Richardson, William, 4, 26
Robinson, G. T., 45, 118
Rubakha, 65
Runaway peasants, 76, 94, 95
Rusalki, 90
Russia. *See also* Soviet Union
    prerevolutionary justice system, 59
    Westernization of, 16

St. Petersburg, 127
Saltykov, Daria, 26
Seeds of Tomorrow, 144
Serfs/serfdom. *See also* Peasants
    banishment to Siberia, 26
    buying and selling of, 24
    crimes against, 27
    establishment of, 3
    flogging of, 26
    given as gifts, 5
    marriages of, 30
    ownership of, 19–20, 24, 25
    price of, 24–25
    as property, 4, 5
    as prostitutes, 25
    renting of, 97
    rights of, 29
    as slaves, 30

Sexual promiscuity, 80
Sheremetev, Count D. N., 19, 29
Sholokhov, Mikhail, 144
Siberia, 5, 24, 26, 95
Simbirsk, 77
Skoptsy, 89
Slaves/slavery, 2, 4, 30
Slavophiles, 16
Smith, Jessica, 154
Smolensk, 2
Social Democrats, 117, 120
Socialism, Russian, 115
Socialist Revolutionaries, 117, 120
Sokha, 42
Soloukhin, Vladimir, 148, 156
Soul tax, 45
Soviet Union. *See also* Russia
   climate, 2
   size, 1
   topography, 2
Sovkhoz, 146
Spirits, 90–91
Stalin, Josef, 139
Starosta, 11, 14, 54
Starvation, 57
Steam bath, 66–67
   ritual, 70
Stepniak (peasant reformer), 9, 17,
   46, 79, 93, 94, 107, 137
Steppes, 2
Stolypin, F. A., 123
Strumilin, Stanislav, 149
Sudebnik, 3
Superstitions, peasant, 72, 90

Tatars, 2, 3
Taxes, 12, 13, 57
   soul, 45
Tchur, 91
Ten Days That Shook the World, 128
Tikhomirov (writer), 113
Tolstoy, Leo, 34, 67, 72

Tools, agricultural, 36, 42
Tractors, 145
Transportation system, 44
Tsaritsyn (Volgograd), 77, 78
Turgenev, Ivan, 8, 23, 25, 28, 72

Union of Russian People, 123
Upper Volga River, 2
Uspensky, Gleb, 73

Vasili III, 2
Vedmi, 90
Vegetables, 63
Vehicles, farm, 43
Vicker, Ray, 157
Village
   assembly, 11, 13–14
   layouts, 6–7
Vodyanoi, 90
Volgograd, 77
Volost, 109
Von Virukoff (Russian nobleman), 57
Vorontsov, Count, 19

Walk in Rural Russia, A, 149
Wallace, D. Mackenzie, 15, 16, 27,
   37, 81, 85, 108, 139
War Communism, 130, 132
Weather conditions, Russia, 44
Weddings, 69
Western Dvina River, 2
Williams, Harold W., 24, 86
Witte, Sergei, 120
Women, peasant, 51–52, 158
   abuse of, 52
   Russian view of, prerevolutionary,
   13
World War I, 126

Zemlya i Volya movement, 116
Zemstvo, 73, 119
Znakharka, 60